Racing Odysseus

The publisher gratefully acknowledges
the generous contribution to this book provided
by the Humanities Endowment Fund of the
University of California Press Foundation.

Racing Odysseus

*A College President Becomes
a Freshman Again*

Roger H. Martin

UNIVERSITY OF CALIFORNIA PRESS

Berkeley   Los Angeles   London

University of California Press, one of the most distinguished
university presses in the United States, enriches lives around the
world by advancing scholarship in the humanities, social sciences,
and natural sciences. Its activities are supported by the UC Press
Foundation and by philanthropic contributions from individuals
and institutions. For more information, visit www.ucpress.edu.

University of California Press
Berkeley and Los Angeles, California

University of California Press, Ltd.
London, England

Library of Congress Cataloging-in-Publication Data

Martin, Roger H., 1943–.
    Racing Odysseus : a college president becomes a freshman
again / Roger H. Martin.
        p.   cm.
    Includes bibliographical references and index.
    ISBN 978–0-520–25541–8 (cloth : alk. paper)
1. Martin, Roger H., 1943–   2. College presidents—United
States—Biography.   3. Adult college students—United States—
Biography.   4. Cancer patients—United States—Biography.
5. St. John's College (Annapolis, Md.)   I. Title.

LA2317.M278A3   2008
378.1'11—dc22   2007051017
[B]

Manufactured in the United States of America

17   16   15   14   13   12   11   10   09   08
10   9   8   7   6   5   4   3   2   1

This book is printed on Cascades Enviro 100, a 100% post
consumer waste, recycled, de-inked fiber. FSC recycled certified
and processed chlorine free. It is acid free, Ecologo certified, and
manufactured by BioGas energy.

For Susan,
my constant companion and friend
on this journey called life

CONTENTS

ACKNOWLEDGMENTS

This book is not only a personal memoir but also the story of an exceptional group of young men and women, members of the so-called Millennial Generation, who became my friends and college classmates for one semester at St. John's College in Annapolis, Maryland. These students give me great hope for the future leadership of our country and, indeed, of the world. With their permission, I have used real first names and likenesses, the exceptions being students who spoke to me in confidence. In these cases I have altered their identities and used fictitious names.

In writing this memoir, I have violated an important St. John's convention that requires brief comment. Students and faculty at this unusual liberal arts college almost always address each other formally, using Mr. or Ms., for example, followed by a last name. First names and titles such as Professor or Dean are never used in the classroom. However, first names are sometimes used in other contexts, especially when students know each other. To avoid confusion by using formal names when I write about students in the classroom and informal names when writing about them in the boathouse or coffee shop, I decided to use first names in all cases. I hope that older alumni who prefer St. John's convention of formality will forgive this decision.

There are several people I would like to thank for making my time at St. John's so pleasurable and the writing and production of this book possible. It took considerable open-mindedness for Chris Nelson, the president of St. John's, and Harvey Flaumenhaft, the dean in 2004, to allow a sixty-one-year-old college president to enter their college as—of all things—a freshman. It had never been done before! Then again, St. John's is known for defying convention. The support of these two men is deeply appreciated as is the encouragement I received from Anita Kronsberg and Christian Holland, my tutors in freshman seminar. Leo Pickens is a most unusual athletic director and a wonderful coach as well. I am indebted to him for allowing me to live the boomer fantasy of becoming an intercollegiate athlete one last time. Other people at St. John's who were generous with their time and support are Judy Seeger, Rosemary Harty, Gail Griffith, and Susan Paalman.

Dennis Glew, chair of the history department at Moravian College, read the entire manuscript as both a classicist and a 1965 St. John's graduate. His comments about the literature I studied and also about St. John's unique culture were enormously helpful, as were the comments of Rick Clothier, director of rowing and professor of physical education at the United States Naval Academy, who read the rowing narratives for technical accuracy. I would like to thank as well Lisa Bacon and David Bushko for helping to improve critical sections of the manuscript.

My agent, Gail Ross, having read about my sabbatical in the *Washington Post,* was the first to suggest that I write this book; her support is deeply appreciated. Her colleague Howard Yoon's editorial suggestions and comments improved the manuscript in significant ways. I would also like to thank the University of California Press, especially Laura Cerruti, my editor, as well as Kate Warne, Sharron Wood, Lorraine Weston, and Alex Dahne for their parts in making this book a reality.

I owe the Randolph-Macon College Board of Trustees and its chair, Macon Brock, a debt of gratitude for granting me a sabbatical leave in the fall of 2004. They probably thought I had lost my senses when I told them what I planned to do. I hope that the result of their trust in me is a book that contributes to the ongoing conversation in America about the importance of a liberal arts and sciences education.

Finally I must mention John D. Walsh of Jesus College, Oxford, my former tutor, who not only initiated me into the ranks of historians going back to Herodotus and Thucydides, but also taught me how to be a better writer. Over the years, he has been my role model as a teacher and scholar.

Mamaroneck, New York
New Year's Day, 2008

Prologue

It must be three in the morning. I can't tell exactly what time it is because the wall clock in my room at Weinberg, the main cancer facility at Johns Hopkins, is hard to see. It is dark as a cave. I'm constrained, only able to move my head to the left and the right. The city lights, out of sight and five stories below me, are interrupted by eerie shadows cast on the white walls of my room with depressing regularity. Like these shadows, my life, past and present, seems unfocused and unsettled. Am I on a treadmill after spending my entire life in one profession? Is this dark, anonymous room the place where my life will unceremoniously end? I sense that perhaps I am one among many in this cancer ward feeling the same sense of anomie and hopelessness.

I am not very comfortable. A three-pronged catheter has just been placed deep in my chest. Three tubes, one white, one blue, and one red, ascend from the catheter to three bottles hanging from a chromium-plated IV pole next to my bed. This is why I can only move my head. One of the bottles contains Interleukin II, a treatment for advanced melanoma, the cancer I developed at the beginning of the summer. I am semidelirious because of the biological agents streaming into my body. I cannot think very clearly. But, as if I were having a bad dream, I am remembering the events that got me here.

I am remembering the coughing episode at commencement and at the alumni reunion just four months before. I am a college president, and being able to speak clearly is extremely important in my work. I was sent to a pulmonary expert at a nearby hospital. X-rays revealed a disturbing shadow behind my left lung. Susan, my wife of thirty years, cried when the doctor said that it might be a tumor.

The next day a CT scan confirmed our worst fears: there was a three-centimeter tumor on top of my left lung. The doctor told me that this is what was causing the coughing. He suspected that it was a reoccurrence of the melanoma, a type of skin cancer, that had appeared two years before on my left earlobe, and which had been surgically removed. Melanomas are usually brown or black and of irregular shape, but mine was colorless, like an enormous mosquito bite that never went away. At the time, we thought I was in the clear, but the melanoma had obviously come back, this time internally. A painful biopsy determined that, indeed, my skin cancer had metastasized.

As I am remembering these things, a nurse walks into my room and takes my temperature. She then hangs a bottle of Cisplatin on the IV pole and connects the tube to my catheter. She is wearing very heavy rubber gloves because Cisplatin can erode the skin of anyone who touches it. Before she leaves, she makes me drink some water. Alone once again, my mind goes back to the painful events of the past few months.

The only real treatment for melanoma once it enters the body is to have it surgically removed. So just before my fifty-seventh birthday, the top lobe of my left lung was cut out along with the tumor. The surgeon told me afterward that although he got rid of most of the tumor, he did not achieve the margin he likes because the tumor was situated precariously close to my aorta. Since some of the cancer cells might have remained, he suggested that during August I go through interferon treatments, just as a precaution. Interferon is a drug that stimulates the immune system to fight cancer cells.

August was pure hell. Interferon knocked me off my feet. I could hardly make it out of bed each morning. All I had the energy to do was to walk to my office mid-morning, open my mail, and then go back to bed for the rest of the day. I could not eat. Normally 175 pounds, I was down to 140.

The treatment ended the last day of August. A CT scan several days later revealed that the tumor had returned, so we met with my oncologist in Richmond, Virginia. She told Susan and me that I had a year to live, maybe a year and a half at best. She suggested we get our affairs in order and look into hospice care.

The Cisplatin now takes effect. I completely black out.

CHAPTER I

Orientation
(Four Years Later)

"Rusty, you cannot keep putting it off," Susan yells at me from the postage stamp–size kitchenette in our temporary one-bedroom rental in the Bestgate section of Annapolis. The television is blaring, and she is having a difficult time communicating with me. "What will your classmates think if you turn up at seminar not having read the assignment?"

It's mid-August and we have just arrived in Annapolis following a hectic couple of days preparing for my six-month sabbatical. Susan is right. I am once again procrastinating. On this occasion, I have curled up in an overstuffed chair with the TV remote in one hand and a cold beer in the other. I am surfing the channels, searching for the Olympics. My feet rest on a low coffee table, in the middle of which lies a fat copy of Homer's *Iliad,* all 537 pages of it. This is the book I have been reading all week in preparation for the freshman seminar I will be attending at St. John's College. I am behind in my reading, and so I pretend it's not there.

Susan continues to badger me and is beginning to sound like my mother. "You know you are a slow reader. Don't embarrass yourself by failing to complete the assignment."

Susan is making me feel guilty. Only a month previously, Chris Nelson, the president of St. John's College, and Harvey Flaumenhaft, the school's dean, had agreed to let me enter their institution as a freshman so that I could write about the first-year experience from a student's perspective. The idea of allowing a college president to matriculate as a freshman was unorthodox, to say the least, and Mr. Flaumenhaft, for one, had his doubts when I first proposed it to him. He wanted to know why any sane human over the age of fifty would want to do this. Did I *really* want to become a freshman again and hang out with eighteen-year-olds? Did I think that I would fit in? And what about all the reading? Did I really want to read hundreds of pages of Greek philosophy and literature each week? St. John's is the Great Books school, and reading thought-provoking and challenging books is a staple of its academic program.

As I stare at my book on the coffee table, deciding whether to obey my wife or watch TV, I brood over my conversation with Mr. Flaumenhaft. I'm a fairly typical academically oriented guy whose idea of fun is hanging out in a library archive. Does Mr. Flaumenhaft think that I am some kind of eccentric exhibitionist attempting to pull off a publicity stunt? Or that I am just certifiably nuts? And what about all the reading? Do I really want to read ancient literature all day long? What have I gotten myself into?

I put these questions out of my mind and decide to watch the Olympics *and* read the *Iliad* at the same time. Susan looks dubious as I slowly pick up the *Iliad* from the coffee table and begin reading Book 23.

Against the background noise of an Olympic boxing semifinal, I am reading that Achilles, commander of the Greek Myrmidons, has just buried his best friend, Patroclus, recently killed at the hands of Hector, leader of the Trojans and archenemy of the invading Greeks. It is decided that an athletic contest will be held to honor Patroclus's bravery. The orders are startlingly clear: fighting will stop and the soldiers will engage in a variety of sports, including boxing, wrestling, archery, foot races, and shot put. I am thinking to myself, how can this be? How can they hold a mini-Olympics in the middle of a horrendous war that has resulted not only in the death of a valued comrade, but also the slaughter of tens of thousands of people on both sides?

A news bulletin flashes across the television screen and I instantly look up from my book. NBC's Brian Williams is reporting that a large number of American soldiers have died in a suicide bombing in Mosul, in northern Iraq. A war that began over a year ago continues to take the lives of thousands of soldiers and citizens alike. And these news bulletins are becoming alarmingly frequent. It then dawns on me. The *Iliad,* written 2,700 years ago, is as much about my world as it is about Homer's. Like the ancient Greeks, America can also play Olympic games in the middle of a war. I wonder what else I might learn about my own times from this ancient literature. Will the material suggest that nothing ever changes in a world that continues to be defined by human misery and suffering? Or will I find hope that somehow the human spirit can overcome the past and that a world free of war might be possible in my lifetime?

Classes begin in just a few days, and I can hardly wait to become a freshman again.

. . .

It's now Tuesday morning, the first day of freshman orientation. I enter the registration area in the foyer of Key Auditorium. To the left is an imposing monument to Francis Scott Key, after whom the auditorium is named. Key, a member of the St. John's class of 1796, penned our national anthem, and, indeed, the first stanza of "The Star-Spangled Banner" is engraved in huge letters on the wall for everyone to see, giving one the feeling that this is a college steeped in early American history. Through the large windows that surround two sides of the registration area I can see the rest of the campus.

Key Auditorium is part of Mellon Hall, whose modern 1950s architecture seems out of place next to the redbrick colonial buildings, several built in the eighteenth century, that dominate the St. John's campus. I'm feeling out of place as well. The registration area is pulsating with eighteen-year-olds, now joined by a balding sixty-one-year-old man with a red beard speckled with gray and the beginnings of a paunch. I am feeling very conspicuous. For one thing, I am much more used to turning up at these events as a college president, greeting the new students, radiating authority and confidence, reassuring parents that their sons and daughters are being left in competent, caring hands. Now, as a freshman, standing alone in the middle of the foyer like an abandoned child, I feel awkward, disoriented, unsure of myself.

As I join the long queue of freshman waiting to pick up their registration packets, a member of the orientation committee, a severe-looking senior, approaches me and says, in a rather deprecating way, "This line is for students only. Parents wait over there." As she says this, she points to a vacant bank of chairs. I don't have the heart to tell her that I *am* a student, and so I sheepishly step out of line.

Not quite knowing what to do next, I wander over to the windows of the auditorium and stand next to the wall engraved with "The Star-Spangled Banner." From this vantage point I can easily see St. John's lower campus. Outside, families are madly scrambling to move their children's possessions from their cars in the parking lots around Mellon Hall into the various residence halls a few hundred feet away on the Quad. Fathers look like packhorses as they haul their children's possessions up the Quad's broad steps. The freshmen have a bewildered look, as though they are happy to finally gain freedom from their parents but wonder what they will do without them.

I cannot completely share their experiences because I will not be moving into a dormitory, but instead living in a rented house not far from campus. But seeing the pandemonium outside Mellon Hall reminds me of a similar August day back in 1961, when my parents moved me into Smith Hall, a freshman men's residence at Denison University. We had driven more than five hundred miles from my home in Mamaroneck, New York. Winding through the rolling hills of Ohio's Licking County, we suddenly saw this small, beautiful university on the horizon. All of my teenage dreams of going to college came together at that moment. The grandeur of the campus buildings. The spectacle of the central parking lot, full of freshmen and their parents moving books, rugs, clothes, and lamps into the residence halls. The excitement of starting a new life, independent from my mom and dad.

The awe and anticipation I felt then is very much a part of my feelings now as I become a freshman a second time. Is it possible to become a student once again after being a college professor and administrator for more than thirty years? Will I be accepted by my classmates? What unexpected adventures await me?

I turn back to the registration table. The intimidating senior is nowhere to be seen, but the queue has doubled and I don't have the nerve to reclaim my original place in line. Perhaps I'll pick up my orientation packet later and get my ID card instead.

I spot Joy, a staff member in the student affairs office, who seems extremely harried trying to manage the chaos. A determined-looking woman, Joy works for the assistant dean, and, among other responsibilities, she is in charge of orientation. When I ask her where I can get my student ID, she gives me a look of disbelief that suggests, "You idiot. IDs are for the real students, not for a sixty-one-year-old college president pretending to be one." Of course, she is too polite to actually say this. But my need for an ID is real. How am I going to identify myself to campus security when they approach me some dark evening hanging out with students?

I have good reason to be concerned. I recall an event that took place in 1986, when I first became a college president. On my first day on the job at Moravian College, I decided just before midnight to sneak down to the amphitheater in the backyard of my house to watch, from behind a large oak tree, the remaining minutes of freshman mixer taking place. Through the dappled shadows of my lookout, I was spotted by an alert campus safety officer, who was probably thinking that I was either a homeless person or, worse, some kind of pervert. And so, as I left to return to my house, I was grabbed by two burly police officers.

"Let's see your college ID," the bigger one said. "I don't have an ID," I replied. "Then who are you?" the other chimed in. "I'm the president," I responded, annoyed at this point. "Right. And I'm Jesus Christ Superstar," the first cop said. I was arrested for trespassing on the spot. I can only imagine what the St. John's police might think when I tell them I'm a freshman. And so I ask Joy once again, this time with a sense of urgency, "Where do I get an ID card?"

Joy directs me down a long hallway leading to a small room next to the president's office, where two juniors are taking photos for the student IDs.

"Hi, I'm Roger Martin. You know, the older freshman," I say as I enter the darkened room, praying that they won't make fun of me.

"Oh, we know who you are," one of them says with a contagious smile, "and we think it's *awesome* that you are coming here as a student." *Awesome* is a word undergraduates use to describe anyone or anything that is either unusual or unbelievable, and clearly I meet both criteria. But her generous welcome is genuine, and I feel greatly relieved. Someone has finally recognized me as a bona fide student.

I now need a parking pass. Because I must live off campus, I will have to commute to classes, and the parking situation around the St. John's campus is hopeless. My two new friends from the photo ID department direct me back to the central registration area and to a table manned by campus security. Great, I think to myself. I can kill two birds with one stone: get a parking pass and also make myself known to the security officers.

I reenter the foyer, grabbing my orientation packet from a now-empty table as I stride toward the campus security booth. An officer with sergeant's stripes on both sleeves of his white shirt staffs the table.

"How can I help you?" he politely asks, probably thinking that I am a parent.

"I'm a new student and I need a parking pass," I respond, showing him my newly minted ID card.

He looks at the card, then at me, and then at the card again, not quite believing what he sees or knowing what to say. He hesitates, obviously not sure about my true identity, and finally says, "Freshmen aren't allowed to have cars."

"But I'm a *special* freshman who is living off campus," I persist, "and I need to commute to campus."

We aren't getting anywhere, and so I am referred up the chain of command to Paul Mikesell, director of campus security, who just happens to be standing at the door of the foyer. Mr. Mikesell, a muscular man with a kindly smile, patiently listens to my story. He is probably wondering why anyone approximately his own age would want to go back to college. But he is a good sport, and he finally gives me the parking pass I need.

Registration preliminaries completed, I exit the north door of the auditorium for some fresh air. I walk a few yards past Campbell Hall and up the stairs that lead to the Quad, the outdoor gathering place for St. John's students. Returning upperclassmen are assembling here, joining in the carnival atmosphere of move-in day. They are the big men on campus. They *own* St. John's, and the incoming freshmen intuitively know this. These upperclassmen—the men, at least—are not here to reclaim their dormitory rooms. The upper classes move in tomorrow. They are here to check out the freshman women.

I remember back to my Denison orientation forty-three years ago and the fraternity men I encountered my first day on campus. Sporting crew cuts and proudly wearing sweatshirts displaying the Greek letters of their respective fraternities on the front, they were helping the freshmen move into the residence halls, giving directions to bewildered parents, wandering around checking out the new arrivals, and generally making sure by the sublime confidence they exuded that you knew who they were. They seemed to me then like Greek gods—erudite, sophisticated, cool—while I felt like an insecure country cousin, inarticulate and unsure of myself.

But hold on. The Greek gods of my past look very different from the Greek gods I am seeing today. Some of these Johnnies look quite normal, wearing jeans and T-shirts and with regular haircuts. Others look quite different, though, with shoulder-length hair, assorted tattoos, and pierced navels and lips. I spot a young man with a black frock coat and long, flowing blond hair coming out of Randall Hall, the college's dining room. He looks more like a nineteenth-century itinerant preacher than a modern college student. A kid with a bright green Mohawk haircut greets him as if they are long lost buddies. Two other young men, engaged in earnest conversation, are seated around one of the several wrought-iron patio tables that furnish the Quad. They have shaved heads and, like the Hells Angels, wear jeans with steel chains hanging from their broad belts. I wonder if they arrived on Harley-Davidson motorcycles. Two young women, arm in arm, are exiting the east door of the Coffee Shop. Each sports a variety of silver rings piercing various parts of her body.

These Johnnies look very different from most college students I know. And they seem proud of their nonconformity. But why am I surprised? St. John's isn't exactly your typical liberal arts college either, at least not since 1937, when it adopted one of the most distinctive curricula in America.

Founded in 1696 as King William's School, St. John's was, by 1784, one of a handful of colonial colleges that served the new nation. It had some stature, counting among its early students George Washington's step-grandson and two nephews in addition to Francis Scott Key. Never a wealthy college, St. John's faced numerous financial challenges over the ensuing years. During the Civil War it was occupied by federal troops and had to close temporarily. Later in the century it adopted a program of compulsory military training in order to augment its depleted finances. In 1886, after almost going out of business again, the college opened a preparatory school for the United States Naval Academy, founded forty years earlier on a plot of land next door. The stock market crash of the 1920s and the Great Depression seemed like the final nail in the college's coffin.

Even in the face of financial hardship, however, St. John's was not about to go under. In 1937 Stringfellow Barr, a University of Virginia graduate who had attended Oxford, was elected president of the college and, along with Scott Buchanan, the new dean (and an Oxford graduate as well), completely revamped the curriculum. They introduced the Great Books program that would turn St. John's from a struggling regional liberal arts college into one of the most distinctive institutions of higher education in America.

As at Oxford, which had an obvious impact on the thinking of both Barr and Buchanan, learning was to be accomplished largely through seminars, tutorials, and labs, with tutors, not professors, in charge. The tutors would be generalists, expected to teach across the curriculum even in areas in which they had little or no academic training. As a consequence, there were to be no academic departments, or even majors. By graduation, every St. John's student would have read the same hundred or so Great Books.

At the center of this uncommon curriculum was the seminar, which would meet twice a week and would be composed of a dozen or so students and two tutors arranged around a large table. Freshman seminar would focus on classical Greek literature and philosophy, including the writings of Homer, Plato, Plutarch, and Herodotus. By their sophomore year, students would be reading selections from the Old and New Testament, in addition to Italian, French, and English authors such as Dante, Rabelais, and Chaucer. The juniors would focus mainly on seventeenth- and eighteenth-century literature, including classics like Milton's *Paradise Lost,* Molière's *Tartuffe,* and Montesquieu's *The Spirit of the Laws.* By their senior year, St. John's students would hit their stride, reading more "modern" classics like Tolstoy's *War and Peace,* Marx's *Capital,* and Dickens's *David Copperfield.*

In addition to this seminar, all students would be required to take tutorials in language (initially Greek, Latin, German, and French), music, mathematics, and writing, plus labs in physics, chemistry, and biology, all based on the Great Books. If this were not enough to keep the students occupied, the college would also sponsor two lectures each week that would be attended by the entire community. On these occasions a faculty member or a visiting scholar would expound on a wider range of books than those found in the canon, or what the community called "The Program." In sum, the St. John's curriculum was a radical—though some might say traditional—expression of the liberal arts and sciences. And largely because of this audacious curriculum, the college began to prosper.

. . .

Wednesday is the second day of orientation, and I have some time to kill. This morning we moved out of Bestgate and into our new home on Franklin Street. Susan decided to drive to Target to buy some household items, so I have most of the afternoon free.

I decide to check out the Coffee Shop, which is located in the basement of McDowell Hall. This is where St. John's students congregate after classes. On a bulletin board just outside the main entrance an announcement catches my eye. "WALTZ PARTY TONIGHT. 10:30 PM IN THE GREAT HALL. LESSONS AT 3 PM THIS AFTERNOON." How cool, I think to myself, for a college with a classical curriculum to organize a social event featuring a classical dance like the waltz.

Arriving at the Great Hall a few minutes after three, I am greeted by a junior woman with a distinct British accent. The handsome room is packed with fresh faces, most of them probably first-year students. An ancient gramophone pumps out loud waltz music. "I'm a special student this semester," I whisper, not wanting to disturb the proceedings or be overheard, "and I have no idea how to waltz." I notice that the men have already moved to one side of the Great Hall, and the women to the other, forming two straight lines facing each other. I feel the stares of a hundred pairs of eyes.

The Great Hall, a sparsely decorated room with broad, hand-hewn oak floors, is the perfect place for dance lessons. The elegant white walls sport the portraits of past St. John's presidents, who stare down in stony silence at the unwary students lined up below.

"Terrific," the instructor yells over the music so that everyone in the room can hear her. "Get in line with the men."

As she says this I remember back forty-three years to my first college mixer in the Deed's Parking Lot at Denison and how terribly insecure I felt on that occasion. I was a spectacle to behold: freckle-faced, red-haired, introverted, and terribly homesick. But there I was, hanging out with my male classmates and bravely surveying all the women I wanted to dance with in the worst possible way. Now these remembrances are coming back to haunt me.

"Okay," the dance instructor continues as she turns her back on me. "Now, men and women converge in the middle of the floor, and choose a partner." Could it get any worse?

As the two lines of students walk slowly toward each other, I join the end of the men's line and move forward with them. Across the room, directly in front of me, I see a diminutive blond with a faint resemblance to my youngest daughter, Emily. My future dance partner is staring at me in absolute horror. I can only imagine what is going through her anxious mind. I'm not feeling great about the situation either.

Fortunately for both of us there are more men than women, and as we move forward, the men's line shifts slightly to the right to better match the oncoming women. To the obvious relief of my intended partner—she will now be matched with a student just to my left—I end up with no one.

Suddenly I notice another freshman standing nearby. He hasn't even tried to join the line, probably scared to death that he might experience what I just did. He has good reason to be concerned. He is a skinny, freckled kid. His blue jeans are far too short for his lanky legs, practically shining a light on his white socks and penny loafers. No self-respecting St. John's woman, certainly not one in tight capri pants and stiletto heels, is going to link up with this kid. He's a nerd.

As the waltz lesson begins, I edge closer and introduce myself. Not quite sure who this older man is, he somewhat cautiously tells me, with a slight stutter, that his name is Sheldon. He then falls silent. I sense that Sheldon feels self-conscious. His hands jammed in his sagging pockets, he is a fish out of water.

I ask Sheldon where he comes from. He tells me that he used to live with his parents in a small farming community north of San Francisco and that this is the first time he has been away from home. In a moment of candor he also confides that he is missing his family terribly. Realizing that he perhaps has said more then he should have, he changes the subject and tells me that he considered skipping this event, making some noise about being more interested in the academic side of St. John's. Sheldon is putting on a brave front, but I can tell by his awkward gawks when couples seductively waltz past him that he really wishes he could be part of the action.

As Sheldon and I talk, I notice out of the corner of my eye the dance instructor approaching us. The students out on the dance floor are twirling away, and clearly there will be no wallflowers in her class. "Why don't you guys dance together?" she shouts out to us, again so that everyone can hear. Sheldon's face turns beet red. Having his classmates watch him dance with a man easily his father's age is all his suppressed ego needs to completely shrivel, so I quickly make an excuse and a strategic exit. I never do learn how to waltz.

. . .

With my photo ID and parking pass in hand, I'm almost a freshman, but not quite. Next I must witness a rite of passage that is the staple of most college orientations. The new students must be officially welcomed by the faculty and the president and formally matriculated into the college. I have presided over this ceremony many times myself during the eighteen years I have been a college president.

Susan returns from her shopping expedition and joins me at Key Auditorium, a concert hall that seats about six hundred people. Upper-class students and parents of the freshmen are filing through the auditorium's side and back doors. The freshmen and the faculty are nowhere to be seen. They are probably somewhere in the bowels of Mellon Hall, robing up for this grand event. The upperclassmen have that look of confidence that says, "I've been here before. I know the ropes." The parents are looking extremely fatigued from moving books, computers, televisions, clothes, and mini-refrigerators into the residence halls all day.

At the last minute, I decide not to robe up for the ceremony because technically I am not matriculating at the college. I am also having a difficult time putting aside my presidential persona. As Susan and I enter the auditorium, I automatically move to where most of the parents are seated.

"But Rusty," she scolds me, "shouldn't you at least be sitting with the returning students?"

Once seated in a row populated by some upper-class students, I begin to wonder about the mechanics of the matriculation ceremony: Will there be a good faculty turnout? Did the building and grounds crew remember to turn on the public address system? Is the lighting right? I've fallen into my old ways. I'm becoming my old self again—a controlling, micromanaging college administrator. I'm obviously neither thinking nor behaving like a college freshman.

The chatter of parents and upperclassmen subsides as the president, followed by the dean and faculty, all in colorful academic regalia, finally enter from the side doors of the auditorium and solemnly march down the aisle. They are followed by all 120 members of the freshman class, who seat themselves in the front rows. The president and dean mount the stage.

President Christopher Nelson is dressed in a doctoral gown with three purple chevrons on each sleeve. He is a stout man in his mid-fifties, of medium height and with light brown hair. A St. John's graduate himself, Chris Nelson has been president of the college for well over a decade.

The president approaches the podium and announces the beginning of St. John's 214th convocation. I feel shivers going up and down my spine, something that always happens to me on these ceremonial occasions. The dean then begins a forty-five minute ritual during which each and every freshman is introduced to the faculty, signs the matriculation book, and receives a Greek lexicon as a gift from the college. Freshmen here are required to take Greek.

The president gives a convocation address about "beginnings," an appropriate topic for new and returning students. He says that we have embarked on a wonderful journey, one that will begin over and over again throughout our lives. This is because even if our journey and the search it entails take us to a secure place as college students—what he calls a "secure landing"—that landing will only be the jumping-off point for another journey, for a further search. The goal of this search, he says, is to return and, for the first time, know the place from whence we started. He cites Homer's *Odyssey* to make his point, suggesting that Odysseus's long journey home from the Trojan War proved to be the jumping-off point for yet a new journey and perhaps a better understanding of himself.

Mr. Nelson ends his oration by citing a verse from T. S. Eliot's poem "Little Gidding":

> We shall not cease from exploration
> And the end of all our exploring
> Will be to arrive where we started
> And know the place for the first time.

The president's words resonate. I, too, have embarked on a journey, a strange and wonderful journey into the unknown. And like most of the freshman, who are now receiving their Greek lexicons, I am scared half to death.

At the reception after the ceremony, Susan and I notice parents saying good-bye to their children, causing me to remember when my parents said good-bye to me after Denison's convocation in Swasey Chapel. I remember how very ambivalent I felt when their car pulled out of the chapel parking lot. They weren't leaving me for just a couple of weeks, as they did when I went to Boy Scout camp each summer. I would not see them again until Thanksgiving, three long months away. I knew deep in my heart that I would miss them dearly.

As Susan and I leave the auditorium, we hear in the distance the Navy Marching Band playing a John Philip Sousa tune. Perhaps the Naval Academy is having its convocation as well.

Later that evening, Susan and I return to the Quad for the first Waltz Party of the semester. I have not yet learned how to waltz, but I wouldn't miss this event for the world. It is 10 P.M., and a multitude of students are hanging around and engaging in animated conversation. Some of the patio tables contain six-packs of beer, but I do not see the kind of binging that we all too often hear about at other colleges. The beer is just a prop. The conversation is far more important.

Susan and I sit by ourselves in the shadows of McDowell Hall, just soaking in the atmosphere. I start to yawn. It's now almost 11 P.M. and the Waltz Party has not yet begun, but the students are having a blast just hanging out.

Soon we spot some upper-class women emerging from Campbell Hall, the residence immediately to our left, dressed to the nines in fancy gowns and accompanied by young men decked out in tuxedos. More students gradually emerge wearing dresses and suits right out of the 1920s. Here comes a kid who looks like John Dillinger, except instead of a machine gun, he is cradling a bottle of champagne in his right arm. He escorts a young woman who looks like a flapper right out of the Roaring Twenties. She is wearing a sequined dress complete with long, white gloves, a feather boa, and a cloche hat, and she carries a long cigarette holder in her left hand. But still, no one enters the Great Hall. Obviously, the scheduled beginning of the Waltz Party has long been forgotten. The students are just enjoying themselves outside in the dark.

It's now almost midnight, and since Susan and I are dressed more like adult chaperones than freshmen, we decide to call it a night.

. . .

Thursday, the last day of orientation, has arrived. My classmates and I have navigated registration and heard from the president. We have also attended our first Waltz Party. We now have three final tasks to accomplish before classes begin: first, to hear about the social and residential life at the college; second, to take a tour of the campus itself; and finally, to enter what Johnnies fondly call "The Temple," where we will meet the college's athletic director and learn about the school's athletic programs.

The residential life orientation takes place in the Conversation Room. Located just off Key Auditorium in Mellon Hall, the Conversation Room is a modern version of a Greek *bouleuterion* (council meeting hall), complete with dark wood columns and a gallery for chairs around three sides of the room. The center of this room, configured as an oval, is now occupied by chairs facing a podium. Above is a skylight that during the day illuminates the room with sunlight. This is where guest lecturers meet informally with the community after delivering the Friday-evening lecture in Key Auditorium, still a St. John's tradition. But the Conversation Room is also just big enough to accommodate the entire freshmen class.

The freshmen have assembled. Seated behind a small podium in front of them is Judy Seeger, assistant dean (a.k.a. dean of students), together with her staff. Ms. Seeger (deans and faculty members are never referred to by their academic title at St. John's) is a graduate of Harvard, where she majored in history, and of the University of Chicago, where she did her doctorate in Romance languages and literature. She has been instrumental in helping me prepare for my time at the college. Even before I arrived, she was alerting her colleagues to the unusual freshman who would soon be in their midst (although I think she forgot to tell campus security). She has also given me some good advice on extracurricular activities, encouraging me to join a choral group (she is a singer herself).

It was also Ms. Seeger who suggested that my true identity not be kept from the students, but rather revealed soon after my arrival. Today, then, she will formally introduce me to the assembled freshmen. Probably not that many of them care who I am, but there has been enough confusion about my identity (at the waltz lessons, for example) that being forthright really makes sense.

I pull up a chair next to a young man wearing a University of Pennsylvania sweatshirt who is sitting alone to the side. He has a pungent body odor, so I can understand why no one wants to sit next to him. He is a tall kid, maybe six feet, two inches, with a spaced-out look that reminds me of a young Albert Einstein. He seems to be so smart that he cannot communicate with common earthlings like you and me. His full head of brown hair is a picture of chaos, and he is generally unkempt. I introduce myself and he reluctantly tells me that his name is Phil, but he doesn't say much more than this, even though I try to engage him in a conversation. Maybe he isn't accustomed to speaking with adults. Maybe he is nervous. Either way, he isn't buying my pathetic attempt to identify with him as a fellow freshman. So I just settle back in my seat and quietly wait for the program to begin, feeling somewhat conspicuous since the rest of my classmates are engaged in animated teenage prattle with their newfound friends.

The noise in the room subsides as Ms. Seeger approaches the podium. She surveys her expectant audience for a minute or so and then begins to speak. She has a voice of authority.

"Before we begin this morning's session, I would like to call on a very special student to introduce himself. Mr. Martin, will you please greet the freshmen?"

As I stand, students turn around in their seats and impassively stare at me. For once in my life, I am almost tongue-tied.

"Thank you, Ms. Seeger," I begin, once I have composed myself. "Well, you all have probably been wondering who this old guy is." My clumsy attempt at familiarity only draws blank stares. "My name is Roger Martin, and while in real life I am a college president, I am joining you this semester as a freshman. Well, not *really* a freshman. But I plan to write about the freshman experience, and I hope to get to know as many of you as I can."

I sit down. A few students nod their heads in acknowledgment, but it's early in the morning, and I sense that my presence has not yet registered with most of them, especially with those who stayed at the Waltz Party until 3 A.M. last night. In any case, my moment in the limelight is over. Once again, I'm just another freshman in the room. Ms. Seeger thanks me and the session begins.

Although St. John's academic program is very different from those at most colleges, the social issues here—matters concerning campus safety and residence life—are pretty much the same. The program begins with Joy talking about dorm life. Apparently, in addition to running orientation, she is also in charge of the residence halls. We are told to respect our roommate's privacy, to always lock our doors when we leave our rooms, and to be nice to the janitorial staff and not leave big messes for them to clean up. Joy then introduces each of the residence hall assistants who are sitting around the room. The RAs are mostly juniors and seniors.

The college nurse is next up. Dressed in a white uniform, she seems very open and compassionate, just the kind of person you would want to go to if you were sick. She gives a few health tips ("Since we can't get flu vaccines this year, be sure to regularly wash your hands") and encourages students to drop by the health center to meet her staff. At the conclusion of her remarks a student wearing a T-shirt with a big peace symbol on the front and who has had his hand in the air for several minutes asks if students can get free condoms from the health center.

There is nervous laughter from the assembled freshmen. This question is a throwback to the previous college generation. They didn't ask about free condoms, they *demanded* them. But these kids are Millennials, and sex is a private matter, not discussed in public. The nurse, who is probably used to this question, says that contraception issues can be addressed by her staff and, yes, condoms are available for the asking in the health center.

We next talk about the *big* topic on college campuses these days—drinking. At the Waltz Party the other night beer was obviously visible, though I saw no evidence of alcohol abuse. No matter. This morning we are lectured by Mr. Mikesell, the security chief who got me my parking pass, not to consume alcohol until we are twenty-one. I can see students rolling their eyes, much as Randolph-Macon students do when I make the same pedantic speech at their freshman orientation. Millennials have heard this sermon a million times since middle school, and no matter what any adult says or how many times they say it, they will, unfortunately, still illegally drink alcohol.

As the session ends, we are divided into groups for student-led tours of the campus. My group is to meet our tour leader, a senior by the name of Don, on the Quad in ten minutes. Twenty-five of us leave the Conversation Room and briskly march through the auditorium foyer, across the walkway, and up the Quad steps. We spot Don sitting on one of the Quad's wrought-iron chairs, chatting with some other upperclassmen.

I had actually met Don several days ago. An affable guy from New Haven who puts you at ease as soon as you meet him, he has been hanging around campus since Wednesday checking out the freshmen. Don is joined by his friend Pat, and together they begin the tour by taking us through the basement of Campbell Hall, where the washing machines are located.

"If they don't work, just give them a swift boot," Don tells the group as he kicks one of the machines. He is very much in charge, and the freshmen are impressed.

We continue through Campbell's basement hallway, and, when we emerge on the other side, we hang a sharp left past Humphreys Hall, where the bookstore is located ("You can purchase any classic in print," Don claims). We then walk past the Greenfield Library, until a few years ago the home of the archives for the state of Maryland.

We are now standing in the center of the college lawn. "This is the heart of St. John's," Don says as he makes a grand, sweeping gesture with his right hand. He does this as though we were standing on the north rim of the Grand Canyon, surveying the majesty of the surroundings. Don points to McDowell Hall about fifty feet away. He tells us that McDowell was built before the American Revolution and is the third-oldest academic building in America. He mentions that it is the center of campus social life, along with the Quad on the opposite side and the Coffee Shop in the basement.

Don continues his spiel as we make our way across the well-kept lawn, past Pinkney Hall, a student residence, and toward Woodward Hall, at the northeast boundary of the campus. As we take the tour, members of my group begin to chat with me. Some heard me introduce myself just a few minutes ago and are curious.

A student from Washington, D.C., asks whether I am living in a residence hall. "No, I'm living off campus with my wife, Susan, and our flat-coated retriever named Angel," I tell her.

"Oh, can I come over and pet your dog?" she asks with a melancholy look. "I miss my dog so much."

"Any time," I say, amazed at how many of these students seem to be missing their pets. "Angel loves to be petted."

A second student, a young man from Oregon with jet-black hair, asks me whether I'm taking the entire course of study. "Primarily the freshman seminar and some extracurricular activities, and only until the end of December," I reply.

A third student, a young woman with purple hair and who is almost as tall as I am, introduces herself as Shannon. She asks what a college president does. "We read lots of memos and raise money," I say, somewhat with tongue in cheek.

As we approach Woodward Hall, Don suddenly points to a bald patch of lawn where an enormous poplar called the Liberty Tree recently stood, until it was severely damaged by a storm and had to be taken down. Don claims that Thomas Jefferson and George Washington plotted the American Revolution under this stately tree.

After passing this sacred spot we enter Woodward Hall, formerly the college library, but now the Graduate Institute where St. John's runs a small Master of Arts program in the classics. Don wonders whether all twenty-five of us can cram into the tiny elevator just inside the front door. I reluctantly go along with the group wondering what Don and Pat will do if the elevator gets stuck between floors. But we safely make it to the top floor, where Don shows us a beautiful seminar room named after William III, patron of the school that preceded St. John's. Don claims that this area is open all night. "Great place to study and sleep," he says, "especially if you can't stand your roommate."

As we leave Woodward Hall, on our way back to the beginning point of our tour, Don dispenses some useful information. "See that parking lot over there?" He is pointing to a lot behind Chase-Stone House, another residence hall. "Campus security doesn't check that area as carefully as they should. So if you are a freshman and illegally have a car, that's the best place to park."

Once again we are approaching McDowell Hall and the northeast entrance of the Coffee Shop. "Want cheap food?" Don rhetorically asks. "The coffee sucks, but the burgers aren't too bad."

Our tour is running late, but for some reason that is not clear, Don wants to return to Mellon Hall. Most of us could probably skip this part of the tour. We have already spent countless hours in Mellon trying to get registered. But as we enter the foyer to Key Auditorium for the umpteenth time, Don points out an older woman briskly walking in the opposite direction.

"See that lady?" he says, muffling his voice with his right hand as she leaves the building. "That's Eva Brann. She's an icon. The St. John's experience isn't complete until you've had her in seminar." He is referring to one of St. John's most celebrated faculty members, an archaeologist of international reputation who is celebrating her forty-seventh year on the faculty. I make a mental note that this is a person I would like to meet.

"Oh my gosh," Don says as he checks his watch. "Mr. P is going to kill me." He is referring to Leo Pickens, St. John's athletic director. Mr. Pickens's not-to-be-missed introduction to St. John's athletic program was scheduled to start five minutes ago.

"Okay. We're going to skip the Mellon tour and jog over to the gym," Don says as we turn around and leave Mellon the way we came in. We all thank Don for his perspective on the college and then start running across the lawn to the gym, which is located on the opposite side of the campus.

All the freshman tours except ours have converged on Iglehart Hall, but Mr. Pickens has patiently waited for us. As we enter the side door of the gym, half out of breath, and into a small reception area, he asks us to remove our shoes as though the gym were recently constructed and he didn't want us to scuff up the new floor. But this is hardly the case. Built in 1910, Iglehart Hall isn't exactly a state-of-the-art athletic facility. It probably looks exactly as it did when St. John's freshmen entered through the same door almost a hundred years ago.

Basically, the building is a basketball court with a wood-beamed cathedral ceiling and brick walls. The gym is too small for bleachers, but circling around the basketball court, maybe ten feet off the playing floor, is a banked wooden track that can be used either for jogging or for spectators when a basketball or volleyball game is being played below. Out of sight, behind the walls, are very modest weight rooms and lockers. The gym has a musky smell that betrays its antiquity.

We sit on the floor in a wide semicircle as Mr. Pickens, a man of modest build but piercing eyes, looks over us in pregnant silence. I sense that we are in the presence of a sage. Mr. Pickens begins to speak, softly at first. He explains that we are not seated in a gymnasium, but rather in a sacred building, what he calls his temple. He talks about how athletics was as much a part of Greek culture and society as political discourse and debate, and he tells us that athletics must therefore be taken seriously and treated with worshipful reverence. Throughout his oration he uses quotations in Greek from Plato and Herodotus, giving the freshmen a sense that somehow what is done here has a symbiotic relationship with what happens in the classroom. He says that although the athletic facilities at St. John's are somewhat limited compared to those of most colleges, participating in almost any type of athletic competition is possible. For those inclined toward something a bit uncommon, he notes that Ultimate Frisbee and croquet are very popular at St. John's. He also tells us that St. John's is the national croquet champion, and the annual spring match with the Naval Academy is an event not to be missed.

Mr. Pickens continues his sermon by saying something quite extraordinary, something you would not expect to hear from an athletic director.

"Skill and previous experience," he says, "are not required here at St. John's, only *thumos*. Passion." As he says *thumos* he lightly pounds his chest. "Everyone who shows up will be on the team. *Everyone.*"

As he repeats this last word, he seems to be looking directly at me, perhaps because I stick out in this sober-faced crowd of youngsters. Mr. Pickens's invitation is meant for me as well.

CHAPTER 2

Hubris

Orientation is over. No more advice. No more speeches. Tonight we attend our first freshman seminar.

I am standing with a large group of Johnnies on the Quad
behind McDowell Hall. The area is illuminated by a full moon.
Frogs can be heard croaking in College Creek, only a stone's
throw away though not in view because the area is shrouded in
a dense fog. I can feel a heightened sense of anticipation from
the chattering crowd, especially from the freshmen. Many of
them are scared to death by the stories they have just heard
from the upperclassmen.

"You have Mr. Manson for seminar?" a sophomore is overheard exclaiming to three wide-eyed freshmen. "He eats students alive who don't come to seminar prepared." I heard the
same scuttlebutt as I began classes at Denison, and it scared me
half to death as well.

The bell rings, and the McDowell mob warily move toward

Mellon Hall, where many of the seminars are held. It's reckoning time.

As we descend the wide steps of the Quad and walk toward Mellon, three more freshmen from my orientation tour group catch up and again begin interrogating me.

"Where do you come from?"

"I live in Ashland, Virginia, just above Richmond."

"Why do you want to become a freshman again?"

"Because I'm interested in students."

"Did you *really* read the first six books of the *Iliad?*"

"Yes, I did. Did you?"

Just before we enter Mellon, the student who asked the last question admits that he didn't finish this evening's assignment and confides that he is terrified what his tutors might say if they find out.

I enter Mellon 101 a few minutes before class. The room is very utilitarian. With a long workbench facing the large windows to the northeast, it looks as if it serves as a physics lab during the day. Tables supporting a random collection of old electrometers have been pushed to the side of the room. In the middle is a large oak seminar table, and around it are twenty-two wood-framed rush chairs that seem designed to be uncomfortable, perhaps to make sure the seminar participants don't fall asleep. On the opposite side of the room, across from the windows, is a large blackboard that takes up half the wall surface.

Already assembled around the seminar table are about fifteen or sixteen students, all looking rather subdued, not knowing exactly what to expect. At one side of the table, with her back to the large window and with the class roll and three translations of the

Iliad placed neatly before her, sits Anita Kronsberg, one of the seminar leaders. She is wearing a very sensible light-blue short-sleeved sweater. In her mid-forties, Mrs. Kronsberg looks to me more like a graduate student than a St. John's tutor.

I had met Mrs. Kronsberg several weeks earlier, when I visited St. John's to plan my sabbatical. She struck me as a caring and competent teacher, very interested in what I was attempting to do, and I liked her immediately. It quickly occurred to me that Mrs. Kronsberg, a 1980 graduate of St. John's, was a college freshman the year I began my teaching and administrative career at Middlebury College. Had she attended Middlebury rather than St. John's, she could have been *my* student. Now our roles are reversed. I am *her* student and, in the St. John's tradition, which requires all seminar participants to address both the tutors and the other participants as Mr., Ms., or Mrs. instead of by their first name, I will have to address her not as Anita, but as "Mrs. Kronsberg."

This tradition has a purpose. Unlike at most colleges, where the instructor is clearly an authority figure to whom students defer, everyone sitting around the seminar table at St. John's, including the tutors, are co-participants. Of course, the tutors open the seminar with a question and eventually evaluate the students, but in class no one is considered superior to anyone else. As a consequence, titles like "Professor" and "Doctor" are dispensed with, turning seminar into a dialogue of equals that Socrates would have been proud of.

But St. John's tutors are different from most faculty in another respect: they are generalists. Like all tutors at the college, Mrs. Kronsberg teaches the Great Books across the curriculum. This is her year to cofacilitate one of the several freshman seminars taking place this evening, but she also tutors freshman Greek and mathematics. The college has avoided the kind of academic specialization prevalent in so many small liberal arts colleges trying to imitate large research universities. The St. John's faculty are truly Renaissance teachers.

Soon the second tutor, Christian Holland, enters the room. Unlike most faculty, who have succumbed to wearing chinos and loafers, Mr. Holland, a man in his early forties with short black hair, is wearing a Brooks Brothers jacket, a stylish tie, and brown oxfords. With his back to the large blackboard, he sits directly opposite Mrs. Kronsberg. A few stragglers come in just behind him, making up our complement of twenty students and two tutors.

The seminar starts precisely at the stroke of 8 P.M. But just as Mrs. Kronsberg begins to read the attendance role, a woman, looking quite frazzled, enters the room. There are no vacant chairs.

"I'm not sure which seminar I'm supposed to be in," the intruder diffidently confesses. "Can I join this one?"

I'm about to give up my seat, feeling somewhat out of place myself. But before I can slide my chair out from under the seminar table, Mrs. Kronsberg proclaims, in a gentle yet firm way, "No, you can't. If you go down the hallway, campus security will be happy to tell you where your seminar is meeting."

I feel badly for this young woman. Just about the last thing an eighteen-year-old wants to do is make an embarrassing gaffe like this in front of her peers. Mrs. Kronsberg, however, is correct in not allowing her simply to join our seminar. College freshmen need to take responsibility for their lives now. Parents are no longer around to tell them what to do or where to go.

Hopefully this young woman has learned an important lesson that will save her from future embarrassments.

I'm wondering how things will proceed. The job of a tutor at St. John's is not to lecture, but only to get the conversation going and keep it more or less on track. So Mrs. Kronsberg asks a simple question in order to break the ice: "How does the *Iliad* begin?"

At most colleges, and certainly in classes with a new group of freshmen, there would be an awkward silence at this point, in large part because first-year students often don't take their reading assignments seriously and therefore have very little to say. Not at St. John's. Almost without pause, the class explodes into conversation. The energy of this epic poem has obviously ignited their imaginations.

Homer apparently wrote the *Iliad* sometime between 750 and 650 B.C.E. We don't know the exact date, or even if a man by the name of "Homer" was the author. It is a story of rage, honor, revenge, and hubris, something all eighteen-year-olds can identify with. The setting is the plains of Troy, on the coast of the Aegean Sea in modern Turkey. Nine years before the story begins, the Achaeans (a collective name for the sometimes discordant tribes that comprised parts of what is now modern Greece), under the leadership of Agamemnon, king of Mycenae, sent an invading force to sack Troy. This was done to avenge the acts of their Trojan rivals who, under the leadership of Paris, had earlier absconded with Helen, the wife of Agamemnon's brother, Menelaus, king of Sparta, forcing her to become Paris's consort. The Achaeans want to reclaim their honor and retrieve Helen in the process. Many allies, including Achilles, commander of the Myrmidons, have joined the invading force, but the invasion has not gone well. There has been a great loss of life on both sides.

Achilles is furious with Agamemnon because of a dispute over the spoils of war. As a consequence, Achilles withdraws from the fighting, at great cost to the Achaean side. He only returns to the field when his best friend, Patroclus, is felled at the hands of Hector, supreme commander of the Trojans and brother of Paris. Achilles takes revenge by killing Hector in bloody hand-to-hand combat and then dragging his mutilated body around Troy in full view of Hector's entire family, including his father, King Priam. Achilles eventually succumbs to Priam's plea for mercy and allows the Trojans to give Hector an honorable burial.

The class responds to the tutor's question. A student who has obviously done her homework points out that the *Iliad* begins with an argument between Agamemnon and Achilles over two women acquired as spoils of war: Chryseis, who belongs to Agamemnon, and Briseis, who belongs to Achilles. Chryseis, she points out, has connections in high places, namely through her father, who is priest to the god Apollo, divine champion of the Trojans. When Apollo sends a plague against the Greeks, Agamemnon is forced to return Chryseis to her father. Agamemnon then demands that Achilles turn over Briseis as recompense. Achilles bristles with rage.

The theme strikes a personal chord with me. I remember how outraged I was twenty years ago when large parts of my doctoral dissertation appeared without attribution in a popular book written by a prominent scholar who earned significant royalties largely because of my labor. Like Achilles, I was angry and frustrated. I, too, wanted revenge. Homer speaks volumes to the human condition.

But I keep this venomous thought to myself for a good reason. Before I joined the seminar, it was agreed that I would observe but not engage in the conversation. Since the students are evaluated on their verbal participation in class, I felt it would be inappropriate for me to take up their time by sermonizing on the literature we would be reading. In any case, I am not here to receive academic credit.

But I have a more personal reason for not participating, a reason I'm not particularly proud of. I am almost clueless when it comes to ancient Greek literature and philosophy. I had no exposure to this literature in high school, and when I took the freshman Western Civilization course at Denison, which featured passages from many of the Great Books we are now reading at St. John's, I ended up with a dismal grade. By not participating in the seminar discussions I won't run the risk of humiliating myself in front of this class of extremely bright teenagers. So I keep my mouth shut and just listen. However, as compensation for this self-imposed silence (and violating an expectation that notes are not to be taken in seminar), I secretly record my thoughts not only about the literature we are reading, but also about how this literature relates to the turbulent world around me.

The discussion continues at a brisk pace, but it is very disjointed and not particularly focused. Indeed, it has fallen far short of the St. John's ideal, which requires parity around the seminar table. Most students are directing their comments to the tutors, not to their fellow students. The tutors, who have advanced degrees, are perceived by the students as experts rather than as fellow seminar participants. Some of the students speak with more frequency than insight; two or three male students particularly tend to dominate the conversation. The women just listen, nodding knowingly at one another as though this kind of behavior is all too familiar to them. One of the men is obviously trying to impress the tutors. He frequently quotes authorities on the meaning of the first few lines of the *Iliad*, but after doing this several times, he is gently reminded by Mrs. Kronsberg that he should stick with the text and give his own opinions, not the opinions of others, another expectation at St. John's.

The students are struggling to remember their classmates' last names. I am struggling as well. I find that I identify each student around the table according to their physical appearance. The female student immediately to my left, whom I recognize from the orientation tour as the dog lover, has a small rose tattooed on her right shoulder. The young man across the table sitting next to Mr. Holland sports an Amish-style beard. Next to him sits an older student who has a shaved head and a number of silver rings piercing various parts of his body, including his lower lip. To my right is a young man wearing a brightly colored shirt decorated with tropical flowers. To his right is a kid who vaguely resembles a younger version of Tom Cruise. He's wearing a soccer jersey with "Chelsea Football Club" emblazoned across it in large white letters. I can only imagine how they are identifying me.

At 10 P.M. sharp Mrs. Kronsberg brings the conversation to a conclusion. It has been intense, and the tutor's intervention to end the conversation is met with silent protest. No one wants to stop. They will have to continue their discussion outside the classroom, perhaps in the Coffee Shop. As for me? By the second hour of the seminar, I had to do everything I could to keep my mouth shut.

. . .

College is not just about academics, but it is also about extracurricular activities. And just like my freshman classmates, I must soon decide how I am going to spend my time outside the classroom. The options at St. John's are almost limitless, and I have received plenty of advice on what to do. This afternoon all the leaders of the various clubs and athletic teams at St. John's will meet with the freshmen to review the many options.

Key Auditorium is packed. Seated on the apron of the stage and engaged in conversation are the club presidents (called *archons* at St. John's) and team captains, the juniors and seniors who will try to recruit the freshmen in the audience. I notice a group of male students from my seminar sitting together toward the back of the auditorium. This is a good sign, because it suggests that friendship groups are being formed around the academic program, not because of membership in a particular social clique like an athletic team or a fraternity, as happens at many colleges. So I find a seat next to the Tom Cruise look-alike wearing the same Chelsea Football Club jersey he wore the other day in seminar.

The presentations haven't begun yet, so I attempt to have a conversation with my newfound friend. All I can get out of him is that his name is Garret and that he comes from a little town outside Pittsburgh. Like Phil, whom I met at orientation, Garret seems uncomfortable talking with me. He sat here to be with his classmates, not with some old geezer who is clearly not a member of his age group.

"What's up, Garret?" I ask.

"Nothin'," he answers in a monotone.

"So what extracurricular activities are you thinking of getting involved in?" I stubbornly persist.

"Dunno," Garret answers, avoiding eye contact.

Clearly uncomfortable with the situation in which I have placed him, Garret turns away from me and starts chatting with someone his own age. I feel silly. I wonder whether I will ever fit in.

The noise in the auditorium begins to subside as the head resident director approaches the podium at the right of the stage. The club archons and team captains remain seated. She announces that each representative will be introduced in turn and then invited to briefly say something about his or her organization.

At most colleges you would expect a political club, a thespian group, the student newspaper, the baseball team, and so forth. But this is St. John's. First up is the archon of the Gaming Club, who says that his organization is dedicated to playing games—any kind of game. Someone in the audience, probably a friend of this young man, jokingly asks whether strip poker is included.

"I said *any* game, nitwit. Don't you understand English?" Everyone laughs.

Next up is a student who introduces himself as a "screwed-up nerd" (he kind of looks like one), but who in fact is archon for an organization called Badly Translated Chinese Stuff. At least that's what I hear from the back of the auditorium. He speaks in muffled tones, so I can't quite understand what his club actually does.

He is followed by a senior in workman's overalls who is archon for the woodshop. He stands up and says, "We make stuff in wood," and then sits down, again to the lusty cheers of everyone in the auditorium.

The captain of the croquet team and several players are greeted next. When this happens, all the archons and team captains sitting on the edge of the stage give the team high fives. It's as though the U.S. Olympic gymnastics team had just been introduced. As Mr. Pickens recently mentioned to us at orientation, St. John's is allegedly the national intercollegiate croquet champion, and these young men and women are as close as you will get to campus heroes.

After the cheering dies down, a couple dressed in what looks like diapers and bibs announce the Children Storytellers Club. The club meets every Thursday evening in the seminar room in Woodward Hall named after William III (the same room we visited on our orientation tour), where members read children's bedtime stories to one another. Pajamas are optional, but cookies and milk are served to everyone who attends.

The next archon announces that her club is dedicated to watching bad movies. She quickly adds, however, that "there might be a movie tonight, but I'm not sure," and then has to admit that she is stepping down as archon in five minutes and so it is up to the freshmen to keep the club going.

I like the crew presentation the best. Five burly guys and one woman (who is also archon of the Environmental Club) talk about the glory of rowing on the Severn River. St. John's has its own boathouse on College Creek, not too far from where we are sitting.

We all get up to leave the auditorium. Still smarting from my rejection by Garret, I am, nevertheless, determined to befriend someone—anyone. I am desperate. I spot Christopher, another member of my seminar, filing out of the auditorium just in front of me. I was impressed with Christopher's well-thought-out contributions at our first seminar, which made him seem more like a mature upperclassman than an eighteen-year-old freshman.

Christopher is wearing a Wheaton College sweatshirt, which gives me an opening to ask him where he got it. Unlike Phil and Garret, Christopher responds to my question with more than a monosyllable. Indeed, he seems happy to talk to me, for which I am grateful. As we walk to the Quad, Christopher tells me that he was very active in his church's youth fellowship and toyed with the idea of attending Wheaton College. "Not the one in Massachusetts," he quickly clarifies, "but Billy Graham's alma mater outside Chicago." Christopher tells me that his friends passed on some St. John's admissions brochures and he immediately fell in love with the place. He feels that his final decision to attend St. John's was providential. Christopher is obviously an evangelical Christian.

"You might find this place somewhat of a challenge," I say. "St. John's isn't exactly a church-related college."

"You've got to be kidding," Christopher responds. "When I went to the first Christian Fellowship meeting earlier this week, there were more than forty students present. That's 10 percent of the entire student population!"

"What did you do?" I ask.

"Well, we had an informal seminar on Luke, and then we prayed for each other," he responds.

"Good for you," I think to myself. Even a conservative Christian can find a niche here, but I find this really surprising. St. John's has been a nonsectarian institution since it began as a proper college in the eighteenth century, and I think older alumni would be amazed to learn that their college also appeals to evangelical Christians like Christopher. It's not altogether clear to me why this is. Perhaps St. John's attracts evangelicals because it is one of only a few nonsectarian colleges in America requiring students to read large portions of the Bible, both the Old and New Testaments. Or perhaps a traditional Great Books curriculum is considered safer for conservative Christians than one that requires students to read books written by more avant-garde and modern authors. On the other hand, I doubt very much that these students will maintain all of their conservative religious beliefs after being challenged by the likes of Hegel and Marx, two authors also in the St. John's program.

As we reach McDowell Hall and the Coffee Shop, I am tempted to suggest that Christopher and I chat over some coffee, but I pull back. After being spurned by classmates twice, I've finally made some progress, and I don't want to overdo it. We say good night, and Christopher disappears into the basement of McDowell. I head home to Franklin Street, feeling pretty good about myself.

. . .

Thursday seminar is about to begin. As I enter Mellon 101, I notice that someone has scrawled in large letters on the blackboard, "Hector's a drag! I love Achilles." Even graffiti at St. John's has a Great Books theme.

As we settle into our chairs, Mr. Holland impresses the class. "Let's see if I've got all your names straight," he says. He then starts calling off the last name of everyone present. When a student arrives late, Mr. Holland momentarily pauses and says,

"And you must be Mr. Jones," causing the student to apologize as he frantically searches for a seat. I bet Mr. Jones won't be late again.

Mr. Holland proceeds to finish the roll call. He has no photographs, no notes, only his memory. But in the process he skips me altogether, even though I'm sitting almost directly across the table from him. Of course, I'm not officially part of the seminar. Nevertheless, my ego has been deflated. My childhood insecurities are haunting me again.

This evening's conversation about the *Iliad* is very energetic. Well into the session, Mr. Holland asks the class what they think Achilles' governing passion might be. This question provokes interesting responses around the table. Some argue that Achilles is driven by rage. They point out that he betrays his allies simply because King Agamemnon, his rival, forces him to give up Briseis. Achilles then calls on his mother, Thetis, a sea goddess with helpful celestial connections, to ensure that his countrymen are defeated on the battlefield.

Other members of the seminar are more sympathetic to Achilles, noting that he seems opposed to this war and just wants to return home. They point out that Achilles is not really an Achaean like Agamemnon, but a Myrmidon, an Achaean ally, and therefore not terribly keen on doing the dirty work of a person he despises, for a people to which he does not really belong, in a war he doesn't really understand. Perhaps regional pride is what drives Achilles. In my own mind, I wonder whether personal loyalty drives Achilles. After all, it's the killing of Achilles' loyal friend Patroclus by Hector that finally brings Achilles back into the fray, and with a vengeance that leads to the final downfall of Troy and an Achaean victory.

The conversation now focuses on Dolon, a Trojan spy caught behind enemy lines by Odysseus and Diomedes, two Achaean warriors who are doing some reconnaissance of their own. After receiving vague promises that his life will be spared if he gives up Trojan military positions, Dolon spills the beans and tells all. The class agrees that Dolon is a disreputable coward, willing to sell himself to the highest bidder. They are shocked, however, when Diomedes summarily hacks off Dolon's head after Dolon betrays his comrades. This atrocity leads to further discussion about war itself. What is the point of this war between the Achaeans and the Trojans? Indeed, what is the point of war generally?

The *Iliad* is one of the most violent books I have ever read. Soldiers on both sides of the conflict wantonly slaughter one another. Heads are sliced off and brains spill out. Iron-tipped pikes rip through stomachs, resulting in intestines falling to the ground. Eyes are gouged from their sockets. Anyone who has seen the first ten minutes of the movie *Saving Private Ryan,* a violent but realistic depiction of the Normandy landing of World War II, will get only a partial sense of what the *Iliad* describes. And what is this war about? It's about the fact that Paris, a Trojan, stole the wife of Menelaus, an Achaean. It's all about pride and honor and blood revenge.

Annie, a transfer from Boston University whose face is turning red with frustration, asks, "How can you justify all this death and misery over a woman? I really can't be very sympathetic to *any* of the characters on *either* side of the conflict, Trojans or Achaeans. Power and glory in this book are meaningless."

Some of the other women nod their heads in agreement. But

Nathaniel, a stocky kid with sandy-colored hair that is prematurely thinning and who sports a beard similar to my own, quickly shoots back, "Wait a second. I disagree. War is part of their culture. How can we sit here in the twenty-first century and judge these people?"

Kristopher, a Pennsylvanian with jet-black hair and side-whiskers and who is wearing a dark suit jacket and a pair of jeans, agrees: "Look, the Trojans stole the Achaean's queen. If this happened in our country, if someone stole President Bush's wife, do you think we would sit around and do nothing about it?"

The class seems evenly divided along gender lines between those who are opposed to this war and those who are okay with it—between the women who would have preferred a more peaceful resolution to the conflict, and the men who are quite happy to see the Greeks and Trojans duke it out. But I'm thinking back to my own college days and the war in Vietnam. Like Homer's courageous Achaeans, many of my college buddies went off to fight an unpopular war in a distant land. They were valiant, brave, and courageous, all qualities that are depicted in the *Iliad*. But, like Achilles, they were not sure why the war was being fought. And like Patroclus, too, many of them didn't return home. Again, I see very real parallels between Homer's era and my own.

The discussion ends with the question, "Is the *Iliad* really an antiwar story?" But Mrs. Kronsberg has to cut off the conversation because we are already fifteen minutes past the end of the seminar. We all get up from the table in unison and once again reluctantly leave the seminar room.

As I walk into the hallway, I spot Sheldon among the crowd of students also leaving Mellon Hall. His seminar apparently takes place three rooms up the hall from mine. He sees me and waves, and I wave back. He walks over.

Sheldon looks pretty much like he did when I met him several days ago at the waltz lessons. He is somewhat disheveled, as though he just got out of bed, and he is wearing the same ill-fitting trousers, white socks, and penny loafers. He has a look of despair on his face.

He sits next to me on a hallway bench. "M-m-m-Mr. Martin, I am so discouraged," Sheldon says with a stutter. "I couldn't g-g-get the reading done last night, and I was just chewed out by one of my tutors for not p-p-p-participating in the discussions. I just don't know what to do."

Wanting to help, I ask him why he is having difficulty with the reading. He admits that he feels overwhelmed by the assignments, not just for freshman seminar and science lab, but for the math and Greek tutorials as well. This is a common problem for many college freshmen, especially those who did not read much in high school. He also admits that he has perhaps spent too much time on the telephone talking to his mother. Sheldon obviously continues to be homesick.

"You'll do fine, Sheldon," I say, trying to bolster his confidence. "But maybe you should limit your phone calls home to the weekends. That way you will have plenty of time to get the reading done." Sheldon is apologetic, seemingly embarrassed about even bringing up the subject with me, but he seems in much better spirits as we leave Mellon Hall.

. . .

I can't sing a note. Never could, even when I tried. This is probably why Ms. Seeger suggested even before the semester began that I consider joining a choral group. St. John's encourages students to stretch themselves and to participate in activities they would ordinarily shun. But her encouragement is also the genesis of a great misunderstanding. Only near the end of my freshman experience do I discover that *all* St. John's freshmen must sing together in a freshman chorus. At the moment, however, I still believe that Ms. Seeger was talking about chorus as a voluntary, extracurricular activity. And, because I'm still looking for a way to get involved with other students outside the classroom, I decide to check out a choral group led by Peter Kalkavage, a popular tutor celebrating his thirtieth year at the college. I am incorrectly told that practice takes place in the Great Hall every Wednesday at 7:30 P.M.

When I arrive at the Great Hall at 7:30 sharp, not only is the chorus already singing—practice started half an hour earlier—but they sound extremely professional. I tiptoe to the back of the room, find a chair to sit in, and pretend that I am only a spectator. Looking down on me somewhat disapprovingly from his perch high on the wall is a portrait of Thomas Fell, president of St. John's from 1886 to 1923. It's unimaginable to me that anyone could be president of a college for thirty-seven years!

Soon a soprano catches my eye and motions to me. At first I can't see her face clearly, but when I put on my glasses I recognize her as the waltz instructor with the English accent who tried to get me to dance with Sheldon. She is vigorously signaling me to assert myself and move up front with the tenors. I try to shrug off her suggestion, but she persists. It seems that this woman's mission in life is to somehow get me involved.

This time I obey her. I leave my seat in the back of the Great Hall and awkwardly shuffle into the tenor's section in the front row. As I do this, Mr. Kalkavage, to my dismay, abruptly stops the rehearsal, walks over to me, and hands me two pieces of sheet music. One is Francis Poulenc's *Salve Regina* and the other Anton Bruckner's *Locus iste.* I am totally embarrassed.

The chorus begins singing again—in Latin! After a few tries I am actually singing the tenor part—a bit off-key perhaps—with nine men and one woman, and I am feeling pretty good about myself. Looking around the Great Hall as we sing, I notice that not all of the sixty or so chorus members are students. A man about my age with a neatly trimmed goatee and pince-nez stands just behind me in the bass section. I wonder whether he is a tutor. A woman across the room looks Susan's age and is wearing a wedding band. I recognize one or two upper-class students. This is obviously a community chorus, involving faculty and staff as well as students.

At about 9 P.M. the rehearsal ends. As the chorus members are leaving I walk up to the director's podium and introduce myself. "I really do apologize, Mr. Kalkavage," I then say, "for being late and for disrupting the practice."

As Mr. Kalkavage stuffs sheet music into his dog-eared briefcase, he says, "No problem, Mr. Martin. At least you came out."

"I suppose so," I respond, "but you need to know that I can't read or sing a note of music."

"Doesn't matter," Mr. Kalkavage replies with a smile. "That is exactly what the community chorus is for. People like yourself, who have never sung before. Did you enjoy the experience?"

"Well, sort of," I respond, trying to seem enthusiastic but not really succeeding. "But I have to admit, it was kind of strange."

I feel welcomed, yet I'm not quite sure that this is what I really want to do for my extracurricular activity. Freshman seminar already takes up my Monday and Thursday evenings. Choral practice would mean being away from home almost every evening. Do I really want to completely abandon Susan? Do I *really* want to sing in a community chorus?

Then a light goes on in my head. "Who am I kidding?" I think to myself. "I'm an over-the-hill jock." At both college and graduate school my passion was rugby. I lived to play the sport, and I looked forward to the fellowship of the boisterous beer parties and the irreverent songfests that took place after the games. But when I graduated, it was all over. From then on, I experienced sports only vicariously and, like most Americans my age, I either watched sports on TV or attended the occasional game in person. I often caught myself fantasizing that I was the guy kicking the winning field goal. But here at St. John's, I can become an athlete once again. I can actually help achieve a great victory. I can kick that winning field goal. What a great opportunity.

I thank Mr. Kalkavage and slink out of McDowell's front door, avoiding at all costs the waltz instructor, who is leaving just behind me.

. . .

My youngest daughter, Emily, decides to spend Labor Day weekend in Annapolis. On the top of her agenda of things to do while she visits is to use the St. John's weight room facilities, since nothing like this is available in her Brooklyn neighborhood, at least not for free. After depositing her dirty laundry at home, we hike over to Iglehart Hall, both of us in our jogging shorts and running shoes.

As we approach St. John's front lawn and pass the Greenfield Library, I begin to worry. What will the other students think? So far they have only seen me in seminar and at orientation meetings. They know very little about me apart from these settings. They have no idea that I am married and have two children. Now here I am entering the campus with a rather attractive young woman on my arm. I don't want them to get the wrong idea, that I'm some kind of aging lothario. I know I'm being paranoid, but the more than thirty years I have spent as a faculty member and college administrator have caused me to create defense mechanisms. I remember with great pain the tongue-lashing I once received from a colleague at New York University for commenting on how attractive the female students were. It was springtime, and I was a young, unmarried college administrator. But she was right, of course, and I mended my ways. But this seemingly insignificant memory is flashing through my subconscious as Emily and I walk up the brick path past Humphrey Hall and the bookstore.

Suddenly I see Don, the tour guide, sitting with a friend on a bench in front of McDowell Hall. He spots Emily and he gives me a thumbs-up, as if to say, "Rock on, old man. And you've only been here two weeks!" I decide that if I run across any more of my new friends, I will make a point of introducing Emily as my daughter.

Once we arrive at the gym, Emily goes to the weight room, but I decide to try my luck on one of the several ergometers, or erg machines, just off the basketball court. Ergs are used to practice rowing, and right now going out for crew is in the back of my mind. Based on what the coach said, I'm a shoo-in. All I have to do is show up and demonstrate passion. Passion, however, doesn't mean I have a clue how to use these machines. After pulling the rope and bar and sliding on the seat for a few minutes, I finally give up and rejoin Emily in the weight room.

At many colleges the weight room is a centerpiece of the campus, complete with Iso-Flex equipment, angled hack squat machines, biangular gyms, climbing walls, and various treadmills and elliptical machines. At St. John's, the weight room is obviously not the college's most important facility. Just off the basketball court, the oblong room contains a few stretch and weight machines, exercise mats, and an assortment of barbells and some exercise balls, but nothing terribly sophisticated. Overseeing the area is an ancient photo of the college's 1889 football team, a band of tough-looking guys wearing leather helmets and knit sweaters without any shoulder pads. They're lounging on the lawn in front of McDowell Hall, near where I just saw Don. St. John's was an early pioneer in American football, and something of a powerhouse in the late nineteenth century. With the advent of the Great Books curriculum, however, big-time athletics fell by the wayside.

Emily is working out on the room's only lateral pull-down machine. Right next to her is Justin, who is doing sit-ups. Justin, the kid from my seminar wearing the brightly colored shirt decorated with tropical flowers, hails from Hawaii. I don't know him at all.

"Emily, I'd like you to meet Justin, my classmate," I say, somewhat emboldened by my recent good fortune in making contact with both Christopher and Sheldon. Emily is visibly embarrassed.

Justin is extremely polite but is at a loss for words. I don't think he envisioned me as the father of someone his own age. He finally says, "Well, we're *sort* of classmates," to make clear to Emily that he really doesn't consider me his buddy, let alone a fellow freshman. Does Justin feel this way because I never say anything in class? Or just because I look different? Emily and Justin silently go back to their exercises as though nothing happened.

Emily and I eventually exit the gym and begin heading for home. She doesn't say a word, and I can tell she is angry with me. As we walk back up the stairs from the lower playing fields and pass through the Quad again, we run into some of my seminar mates playing chess on one of the patio tables. I grab Emily by the arm and pull her over to the group. "Hi, guys," I say, "thought you'd like to meet my daughter, Emily. She's visiting for the weekend." Total silence. Elizabeth, a member of my seminar who seems frustrated whenever the guys hog the conversation, rolls her eyes the way teenagers do when their parents make a serious social gaffe, as I apparently have. The others just stare at me, speechless. Now Emily is *really* angry with me.

"Hi," she says in a tiny voice. We move on.

My attempt at making friends is obviously not working. The harder I try to be like my classmates, the more I stand out. My daughter, whose social skills and sensitivities are sharper than mine, clarifies the situation once we are out of earshot. "Why did you do *that,* Dad?" she asks as if I had just pushed her down a flight of stairs. "Stop trying to be cool. You're not a teenager anymore."

I am mortified. Emily makes me wonder whether perhaps I should check my adolescent behavior and act my age. On the other hand, if I behave like a college president, I will make very few new friends.

. . .

I must finally decide on an intramural activity. The revelation I had immediately after chorus practice suggests that I should do something athletic, and, indeed, the crew presentation the other day has piqued my interest.

Crew attracts me for at least three reasons. First, I have fantasized about rowing ever since my eldest daughter, Kate, competed in a lightweight boat at Tufts University. I spent many pleasant weekends watching her row on rivers and lakes in New England, and finally saw her race at Henley in England, in one of the world's preeminent regattas. Second, crew would provide an excellent opportunity for me to meet students, especially since I am not living in a residence hall. Finally, I find the crazy idea of racing in a boat with undergraduates curiously appealing. I'm not really sure why this is. As I mentioned, I'm something of an introvert, whose idea of fun is hanging out in a library. But as the president said in his convocation address, this is a time for new beginnings.

The next morning I drop by the gym to meet Mr. Pickens, the athletic director who seemed to be addressing me directly during orientation when he invited the freshmen to go out for a sport they had never done before. Mr. Pickens is also the crew coach.

Leo Pickens, or "Mr. P," as some of the students affectionately call him, is a slight man with a two-day growth of stubble on his hawklike face. He has piercing eyes that seem to say, "I'm a no-nonsense person so, please, no bullshit."

I knock on his door and enter. Mr. Pickens's office is a cub-byhole just off the entrance to the gym, where students are required to take off their shoes before entering "The Temple." His office looks like an academic version of a Bennigan's or T.G.I. Friday's, with all sorts of interesting artifacts on the floor, walls, and ceiling. Facing each other are two battered desks, one of which is Mr. Pickens's. Facing his desk is an old-fashioned barber's chair. Hanging from the ceiling is a sail from one of the college's racing dinghies, placed in such a way that if the roof leaks, water will not spill onto Mr. Pickens's desk. On the wall farthest from the door is a pair of crossed oars, suggesting that this man is also the crew coach. The other walls are crowded with pictures and knickknacks, in-cluding photos depicting former teams, lacrosse sticks, and fencing masks. An old bookcase contains an eclectic collection of well-read paperbacks, including David Halberstam's 1985 *The Amateurs,* the title of which pretty much sums up the ath-letic program here at St. John's.

After I introduce myself as a college president who is spend-ing the next few months as a St. John's freshman, Mr. Pickens just nods his head. He is a man of few words. "What I would like to do," I continue, "is to go out for crew and maybe row in an eight-man boat."

There is a long pause as he looks me up and down, probably wondering whether I am in my right mind.

"Very interesting Roger," he finally says, apparently unim-pressed with the anomaly standing in front of him. Mr. Pickens could not care less whether I am a college president or, indeed, president of the United States. After another long pause he continues, "Maybe we can introduce you to rowing in a single scull. That way you don't have to get up so early for practice."

By ignoring my original suggestion, Mr. Pickens is obviously trying to tell me that no one over fifty should even dream about rowing with high-energy teenagers.

"No," I insist, with uncharacteristic hubris. "I would prefer to row with a team. I'm trying to be a college student again, and being alone in a single scull will not do it for me."

"Okay," Mr. Pickens says with a shrug, not quite sure what to do with me. "We'll see how you work out. Be at the boathouse tomorrow by six."

"Six in the *morning?*" I ask in disbelief.

"You heard me, six in the morning."

I think to myself, maybe I *am* crazy.

CHAPTER 3

Homesickness

It's six in the morning, and I have entered the basement of the boathouse, a large garagelike affair that smells of turpentine and fresh paint. About sixty students are standing motionless, like the living dead, in front of two large garage doors that open out to the docks and College Creek.

Very few of us are totally awake. Eyes are glazed and unfocused, probably from late-night attempts to catch up on weekly reading assignments that are considerably heavier here than at most colleges. For me, getting up at this time is normal. Like many college presidents I'm an early riser, taking advantage of the quiet early morning hours to get much of my work done before the normal day starts. After 9 A.M. my life is like a dentist's—a series of half-hour appointments, sometimes doling out pleasure, sometimes pain.

I recognize some students—Julie, Annie, Christopher, and Justin—from my freshman seminar. Across the boathouse I see

Victoria and Morgan. And I'm pleased to see Sheldon. Good for him for coming out.

Coach Pickens asks the group to sit in a semicircle at his feet. He is a modern-day Socrates dressed up in blue quilted coveralls like those the Chesapeake watermen wear when they go crabbing, a red sweatshirt that says "Johnnies" in big white letters splashed across the front, and a nondescript but well-worn baseball cap. I suspect he knows what is going through our minds at this very moment. We are all wondering why anyone would get up this early in the morning for two hours of punishing physical exercise, often made harder by foul weather. His mission, then, is to convince the students at his feet that rowing is both virtuous and pleasurable.

"I can promise you," he preaches to us, "that being out on the Severn at dawn on a crisp fall morning, watching the sun rising from the east and the geese flying to the south as eight oars move in perfect unison over glistening water, is about as close to heaven as you will ever get in this life." I'm sold. I am also anxious to get out on the river.

Coach Pickens moves on to more practical concerns. Many of us are novices—we have never rowed before—and so he begins with the fundamentals. "Be alert at all times. If the shell capsizes, stay with it. Don't try to swim to shore. Use the oars as flotation devices." A pause. His tone goes from stern to harsh. "If you are going to do crew, I expect you to be present Tuesday through Friday at six every morning, pronto. No exceptions. No absences. Period." We all get the message.

Coach Pickens asks for volunteers to row immediately. I am tempted, but I hold back, not wanting to take the place of a real student. A group of novices leaves the boathouse following Mike van Beuren, the assistant coach, like he's the Pied Piper. Mike has the trim and fit physique of a rower. He also looks to me as if he could be Coach Pickens's brother. My compatriots will practice under his direction in a sixteen-person barge that is tied to the dock.

Another group, whom Coach Pickens calls the "grizzled veterans" because they have rowed before, takes down two eight-man shells from the storage racks. They will row on the Severn. Those of us who remain in the boathouse climb on the ergs next to the garage doors to learn proper rowing technique. I realize how silly I must have looked when I tried out one of these machines during my excursion to the gym with my daughter Emily the other day.

As I practice on the erg, a little ache in the small of my back starts to spread. I haven't even gotten on the water yet. Still, I feel pretty good that my form seems decent enough not to draw any negative comments from the coach. Several other students don't fare quite as well.

We end the session with a thirty-minute video on rowing. Coach Pickens makes a point of getting a chair for me as the others sit on the floor. "Privilege of age," he says. I try to protest, but he just gives me a sly wink.

Later in the morning, as we help the two groups of veterans carry their shells and oars back to the boathouse from the dock, I try to strike up a conversation with Victoria, another student in my seminar. Tall, with dark hair, she seems very serious and intense. Sweatshirts seem to have become my entrée to conversation, and I notice that Victoria is wearing one that says "Hopkins."

"Are you from Baltimore?" I ask.

"No, I'm from Connecticut," she replies, avoiding eye contact.

"Oh, I thought you were from Baltimore because that's where Johns Hopkins is," I persist, seeing that I'm not really making a connection.

"No, Hopkins is my school," she says, as though I asked a really stupid question. It then dawns on me that her sweatshirt is from Hopkins, the elite boarding school in Connecticut, not Johns Hopkins, just up the road in Baltimore, where, not too long ago, I was a resident under rather difficult circumstances.

"What are you doing here?" she asks, just when I'm thinking that our conversation has ended. The introduction Ms. Seeger made at orientation, explaining to the freshmen who I am, apparently had not registered with some students, and so I tell her about my project.

"How do you like St. John's?" I ask as a follow-up, trying to keep the conversation going.

"Okay . . . I guess," she responds with a somewhat puzzled look, suggesting that it is none of my business. Perhaps later I can get to know Victoria better, but now we have to pick up the *Paul Mellon,* a shell named after the same benefactor for whom Mellon Hall is named, making it difficult to continue our conversation.

My first practice ends somewhat ingloriously. All I have done is row on land, watch a video, and help lug a shell back into the boathouse. But all these preliminaries have whetted my appetite. This is the sport I want to do.

. . .

This evening we begin our discussion of the *Odyssey,* Homer's sequel to the *Iliad.* The book tells the story of Odysseus, warlord of Ithaca (and nemesis of Dolon), and his challenging ten-year journey home after the fall of Troy. He and his crew travel the breadth and width of the Western Seas, zigzagging hither and yon according to where the (often god-ordained) winds blow them, sometimes making good choices, but often making bad ones. Along the way Odysseus encounters the fabled one-eyed Cyclops, overcomes the seductive music of the Sirens, narrowly escapes the man-eating monster Scylla and the whirlpool Charybdis, loses his entire crew in a monstrous storm (punishment by Zeus because Odysseus's men feasted on the sacred ox of the sun god, Helios), and ends up shipwrecked on the island of Ogygia, the guest of the goddess-nymph Calypso, with whom he lives for seven years while pining for his wife and family. Eventually freed by Hermes, son of Zeus and messenger of the gods, Odysseus arrives home to his father Laertes, his wife Penelope, and his son Telemachus. His wife has been mistreated by several Ithacan noblemen who have been squatting on his lands and living in his home during his long absence, and for this egregious act of disloyalty and incivility, Odysseus and his son wreak a bloody revenge, killing more than one hundred offenders.

The Odyssey is as much a travel story (Odysseus spends ten years traveling more than 5,000 nautical miles to return home to Troy) as it is a story of new beginnings and self-discovery. And it is a story I can identify with. Like Odysseus, I am on a voyage, racing home after battling with melanoma, no longer sure what I will find when I get there or indeed what "home" means for a sixty-one-year-old college president nearing the end of his professional career. Until my life almost ended four years ago, I was a man with a mission, focused on leading a small liberal arts college into the twenty-first century. I traveled the country on one fund-raising trip after another, apart from my wife and children for long periods of time. When I was on campus I was available at all hours of the day and night to faculty, students, parents, and alumni. And in control—I was always in control. I can really empathize with how Odysseus must have felt being so far away from his family for twenty long years, not seeing his son grow up, and missing his family and friends, because, in a nutshell, this has been my own existence for the past eighteen years as well. But now, like Odysseus, I am homeward bound. The great battles of my life are in the past, and I am wondering what my journey will be like before I arrive at my final destination.

As I am having this thought, I notice that the class is uncharacteristically quiet. Mrs. Kronsberg has just asked us if Penelope, Odysseus's long-suffering wife, represents the Greek archetype of the virtuous woman, resigned, submissive, and faithful to her husband and family. A potentially contentious issue is up for discussion, but for some reason, no one is talking. Everyone is waiting for someone else to answer the question. The silence is deafening.

At another college the professor would start lecturing just to relieve the silence in situations like this. The hallmark of most colleges is the lecture system. Professors speak. Students passively listen and take notes. But at St. John's the job of the tutor is not to lecture, but instead to encourage the students to analyze the texts for themselves.

The students are getting fidgety. Mrs. Kronsberg finally repeats the question, "Come on, folks, what's your opinion?"

Morgan is having none of this. A brooding Welshman with

ruffled jet-black hair, Morgan looks like a young Dylan Thomas. Suddenly, he indignantly speaks up. "What do *you* think, Mrs. Kronsberg?" I understand Morgan's frustration and hear his unspoken subtext. "You're the expert, Mrs. Kronsberg, not me. You tell *me* what this is all about." But Mrs. Kronsberg isn't about to abandon her role as seminar leader, and she does not give in to Morgan's stormy challenge. The awkward silence lingers on for a few more seconds.

Elizabeth, the young woman I tried to befriend in front of my daughter, Emily, lobs in a hand grenade. "I don't know about submissive women, Mrs. Kronsberg. All I can say is that women *always* get a raw deal in Homer's books. Odysseus and his cronies are a bunch of macho slobs. As far as I'm concerned, Homer is a misogynist." Elizabeth is no doubt reflecting on the fact that while Penelope waits for her husband's return, Odysseus is having his way with Calypso on the Isle of Ogygia.

The silence has ended. There are others in the class who are very attuned to gender issues, perhaps mindful of the fact that there are very few books by women in the St. John's curriculum. I have noticed that whenever the topic gets around to Olympian-scale male chauvinism, as only Homer is capable of writing about, it's only a matter of time before these women speak out. The class then explodes into a conversation about the sexual politics of the *Odyssey,* half arguing that Odysseus is not a misogynist, the other half supporting Elizabeth's opinion. I sense that both tutors knew that it was only a matter of time before this conversation would get started. No one needed to lecture.

All of this give and take is actually an important pedagogical tool. The students are forced to analyze the text, to pick it apart and try to make sense of it. This skill will serve them well when they leave school and become leaders in a competitive and increasingly complex society.

Seminar ends at 10:30, half an hour late, and I am worried that Susan will be wondering where I am. But as I leave Mellon 101, I again spot Sheldon coming down the hallway, flapping his arms like a seagull on takeoff, trying desperately to get my attention. "Mr. Martin," he stutters, "can we get together? I need to talk to you. I don't want to impose."

I assure Sheldon that getting together wouldn't be an imposition at all. "Let's have lunch in the Coffee Shop tomorrow at noon," I say. He seems relieved, and I'm excited because I am beginning to connect with some of my classmates.

.   .   .

Mr. Pickens's rhapsody about "being out on the Severn at dawn on a crisp fall morning" was apparently only partly successful. This morning crew has dwindled from sixty to about forty-five stalwarts. I can't blame the no-shows. Getting up at 5:30 in the morning is next to impossible for teenagers accustomed to sleeping until noon. And who needs the aching muscles that come with two hours of rowing? But my resolve pays off. I finally get to row this morning.

The sunrise over the Severn is indeed a spectacle to behold. Primed by the erg machines, we novices staunchly march down to the dock and climb into a sixteen-person training barge. As we row up and down College Creek, the epic poetry of Homer's *Odyssey* provides a balm for the pain I'm again feeling in my lower back.

When young Dawn with her rose-red fingers shone once more
we hauled the vessels down to the sunlit breakers first . . .

The crews swung aboard, they sat to the oars in ranks
And in rhythm churned the water white with stroke on stroke.

(Homer The Odyssey *4:648)*

And churn the water we do, in a boat vaguely similar to the *pentekonters* that took Odysseus and his crew to the ends of the world. I sit in the first position, on the port side of the barge, and directly in front of me sits Sara, an eighteen-year-old freshman.

Sara is a tiny woman, probably weighing no more than ninety pounds. Her arms and legs are as thin as beanpoles, making me wonder whether she has the strength and endurance to eventually race in an eight-person shell or even a single scull. Big glasses make her look extremely smart, which I imagine she is. I just can't believe she is going out for crew. But then again, who am I to wonder about these things?

As soon as we are settled, with sneakers fitted into the shoe straps on the floor of the barge, the assistant coach, Mike, calls from the tiller, "Everyone in the catch position, oars squared and buried." Not knowing what the catch position is, I lean back as far as I can (which is not very far because of my back problems) as the more limber Sara leans forward. The result is a loud clunking of heads and a huge splash as we try to disengage our oars.

Probably feeling sorry for the piteous physical specimen before him, Mike gives me a disapproving look, but otherwise he doesn't say anything. He may be wondering whether this will happen to him in a few years.

As we row up and down College Creek—we are too inexperienced to row in the Severn River yet—I begin to feel queasy.

As a youth, I raced ocean-going yachts on Long Island Sound and never got seasick. But as soon as I turned fifty, seasickness became (to stick with Homer) my Achilles' heel. I turn my focus to the fundamentals of rowing and, by the time our barge returns to the dock, Sara and I are rowing quite well together.

When I finally get home, I immediately call my niece Megan. A freshman at Denison, she is doing what I did forty-three years ago, though with much more success. She is thriving at her new college. We agreed that during my sabbatical we would stay in touch and trade stories. I am extremely interested to know how Denison has changed since I was a freshman there. But I have a more immediate reason to call her. All through high school, Megan did crew and, like my oldest daughter, Kate, she knows the ropes. Right now I need comfort and advice.

As I punch in the number to her cell phone, my back, my hands, and even my fingers ache. She answers almost immediately, and I am relieved to hear her familiar voice. "Give me some hope, Megan," I whine. "I'm aching all over."

Before I can go into detail, she says, "I've decided to drop crew, Uncle Rusty. Practice is too early in the morning for me. I'm going to do something more reasonable and less physical. So I won't be much help. Sorry."

I begin to think that my nineteen-year-old niece is a whole lot smarter than I am.

.   .   .

Not wanting to be late for my lunch with Sheldon, I arrive at the Coffee Shop a few minutes before noon. The Coffee Shop is a pleasant area comprised of three rooms: to the southwest, a large room with an enormous fireplace and wooden tables and chairs; in the middle, a cafeteria and mailroom; and, in the northeast, a dining room with tables and booths. All three areas are empty, but behind the counter in the cafeteria I see two of my seminar classmates, Justin and Elizabeth. They are on a financial aid plan that requires them to work at a campus job. I wave to both of them. While Elizabeth works on brewing coffee, Justin fries onions for the hamburgers they will soon be serving. I recall Don's laconic comment during the orientation tour: "The coffee sucks, but the burgers aren't too bad."

I find a booth in the dining room where Sheldon and I can talk with some privacy. As I sit down, Sheldon appears right on time. He offers to pay for lunch, but I insist that it's on me. Sheldon doesn't refuse, and he orders a double cheeseburger with two huge pickles, a large serving of fries, an enormous chocolate-chip cookie, and a large mug of coffee. "And pile on the fried onions," he calls to Justin. For a skinny kid, he sure eats a lot. Heeding Don's warning, I skip the coffee and order a single slice of pizza and a small Coke. I leave a generous tip.

Sheldon settles into the booth and almost immediately launches into his epic story, completely ignoring the meal in front of him. He is Homer telling me a version of his own odyssey. Like Odysseus, who initially feigned madness to avoid leaving home to fight in far-off Troy, Sheldon didn't really want to travel all the way from his home in California to attend college on the East Coast. But his mother and father, staunch Presbyterians, had their hearts set on sending their son east, in large part to protect him from what they perceived to be the ultraliberalism and godlessness of California's universities. Sheldon tells me that he tried to convince his parents that a college closer to home would have been better, but he lost the argument. So, like Odysseus traveling to the other side of the world, Sheldon dutifully packed his bags and traveled far to do battle with his dual nemeses, shyness and insecurity. And like Odysseus before him, all he could think about was returning home to his family.

It was apparent to me when I first met Sheldon at the waltz lessons that he was having a difficult time adjusting to college. Like me, he doesn't fit the image of a typical Johnnie. He seems out of place, both physically and intellectually. An almost emaciated-looking kid who stutters when nervous, Sheldon looks and dresses as I did in the 1960s. Johnnies lean toward "working-class chic," wearing cargo pants or jeans that look as if they were bought from the Salvation Army but in reality come from Abercrombie & Fitch or Urban Outfitters and cost a small fortune. Sheldon, on the other hand, wears light-gray chinos that look like hand-me-downs from a shorter cousin and an Oakland Raiders football jersey. Any urbane Trojan would immediately identify Sheldon for what he really is: a down-home Ithacan hick.

Like his parents, Sheldon is a devout Christian. Unlike them, however, he sees St. John's—despite its ecclesiastical-sounding name—as a kind of academic Sodom and Gomorrah. I ask him if he knows about the college's Christian fellowship group that Christopher told me about during orientation. Sheldon pleads ignorance. I sense that he has not been looking very hard for fellow believers.

"I just wish," he says, continuing to stutter, "that my classmates here were a bit friendlier." Sheldon tells me that his roommate, who comes from Philadelphia's Main Line, hasn't helped matters. "He is into *everything* and has little time for me.

I hardly ever see him. Even the girls turn me off. I don't know what it is. They all just seem too worldly and intellectual."

I decide to change the subject. "I saw you at crew the other day," I say.

"Yeah," he replies, "but I don't think it's for me. Mom says it's bad for my asthma. And besides, who wants to get up at 5:30 in the morning?"

"I understand," I say. "It's not easy for me either." Knowing from recent studies as well as my own experience that students who get involved in extracurricular activities tend to be happier at college, I suggest that he replace crew with some other pursuit.

"Maybe I will," he says. "I'm thinking about joining the Melee Club."

"What's *that*?" I ask.

"Well, you know how in the *Iliad* there are pitch battles with swords and spears on almost every page, and people kill each other left and right? Well, they've got a club here whose members do battle every Wednesday morning on the playing fields using foam swords, battle axes, and clubs. What they do is really cool." And a little weird, I think to myself. But so what? Who's to say being sixty-one and crashing oar blades in a barge with freshman novices isn't just as weird?

I ask Sheldon how he feels about being so far from home. I have observed that students who have adapted well to their new college environment sometimes forget about their family altogether. They are simply too busy with studies and their new friends to call home. Sheldon, on the other hand, has few friends and is not doing well academically. As a consequence, he spends far too much time on the phone with his mother, a possible sign of depression. On the other hand, Sheldon doesn't seem to mind the time he spends talking to his mother. Indeed, he tells me how much he appreciates the fact that she is so protective of him.

Just listening to Sheldon brings back memories of when I left my home for a faraway land long ago. Our journeys are very similar. His was a 3,000-mile trip from San Francisco to Annapolis, Maryland. Mine was only a few hundred miles from Mamaroneck, New York, to Granville, Ohio. But for both of us, going to college was like traveling to the ends of the earth. Almost from the moment my parents left after opening convocation at Denison, I felt the kind of fathomless void that Sheldon is describing here in the Coffee Shop. And because of this void, I too didn't say much in class, since all I could think about was my family and Thanksgiving break, when I would return home, if only for a week. I remember Mr. Cunningham, my Western Civ professor, calling me into his office the third week of classes and telling me, just as Sheldon's tutor recently told him, that my participation in discussions was lacking and that if I didn't keep up with the work, my grades would suffer.

For both Sheldon and me, going to college was—and is—a modern-day odyssey, and not just because of the distances we traveled. I had never thought of the *Odyssey* in this way before, but the story is in part about homesickness. Like Sheldon, Odysseus is close to his family, and he wishes he never left them. And when the war is over, homesickness compels him to return home, despite all the trials and tribulations he must endure before he is finally reunited with his loving family.

Sheldon is talking a mile a minute. I try to slow him down so he can eat his hamburger and French fries, which are now cold.

He clearly has needed a sympathetic ear, and I have enjoyed playing this role, a role that comes more naturally to me than being a college freshman.

As we get up to leave, I notice that the Coffee Shop is now jam-packed with students, many of them familiar faces both from seminar and crew. What a great place, I think to myself, to meet these kids at a more personal level. I decide to spend at least two days a week hanging out here so that I can get to know more of them. "Hanging out," as I know from my daughters, is what college students do.

.   .   .

Sept 21 ?

As fall approaches, the days get darker and colder. This morning, as I leave for crew practice in my blue Polartec jacket and matching wool knit cap, I look like a dockworker or, worse, like a well-coordinated street thug.

As I walk up the front lawn of St. John's in the pitch dark, I spot three female students in front of me walking toward the boathouse several hundred yards in the distance. Bundled in sweats and bouncing along in running shoes, they talk nonstop. As I follow them down the steps of the Quad, one steals a glance over her shoulder. They immediately quicken their pace, doubtlessly wary of this bearded man who has materialized behind them. I'm not feeling very good about the situation either. The idea that I'm being perceived as a dirty old man rather than a distinguished college president and father of two bothers me now, just as it did when I walked across the campus arm in arm with my daughter.

I can no longer see their faces, just the backs of their hooded heads, but they have stopped chatting and are now almost running to stay ahead of me. It is a startling reminder that women often don't feel safe on college campuses, especially when it's dark. How many times have delegations of women appeared in my office at Randolph-Macon concerned about bad lighting on campus walks, or the need to install emergency call boxes, or complaining about the occasional trespasser? Now I'm feeling like a trespasser myself.

Suddenly a bright beam of light flashes in my face, startling me. Blocking my path are two campus security officers. Remembering the similar incident that took place many years ago when I first became a college president, I instinctively dig deep into my trouser pocket, searching for the student ID I worked so hard to get during orientation. Both men stare disapprovingly at me, as they might a pervert making trouble for the college's female students.

"Hi," I say, trying to seem cool. "I'm a new student here, just walking over to crew practice." I flash my photo ID.

"Oh, you're the oldie," an officer about my age sporting a handlebar mustache says, redirecting his flashlight onto my photo.

"We've heard about you," the other officer, a younger man, says. He sticks out his hand to shake mine as if he is rooting for me.

When I enter the boathouse about ten minutes late, Mr. Pickens is making boat assignments. Last in line, I end up in a coxed four, a boat with four rowers, each using one oar, and a cox. I am assigned the bow position; Christopher, still wearing his Wheaton College sweatshirt, sits in front of me in the number-two position; Julie, also from my seminar, is at number three; and a junior woman I don't know is at stroke, the number-four position. Coxing our four is none other than Sara, the diminutive freshman whose oar I fouled in the barge just the other day.

In a coxed four like this, each member of the crew has a special role: The cox is the strategist. Stroke is the catalyst, the athlete who establishes a sense of rhythm and form for the others to follow. Numbers two and three are the boat's engine room and the strongest rowers. Bow, the position I am in this morning, is supposed to give the boat balance. I'm not sure I'm the best choice for this assignment.

At Sara's command the four of us walk to the rack where our shell is stored upside down. We instinctively follow her orders. Sara has morphed from a novice like me into an accomplished cox.

"Now," she barks out in a shrill soprano. "Lay hold of the boat. To shoulders, ready up." The four of us place our hands on both sides of the shell's gunwales and gently lift it off the rack and push it up to our shoulders.

"Now, over heads, ready up. Now, walk it out." We push the boat over our heads and gingerly walk it through the large doors in the front of the boathouse, careful not to slam into other shells hanging from the ceiling. "Now, to shoulders, ready down." We lower our shell once again to our shoulders.

So far so good. But how did Sara learn to do this so quickly?

As we approach the launching dock on College Creek, Sara barks out, "Weigh enough." In crew speak, "weigh enough" means stop. We obey her orders.

"Now, hands in. Toes to the edge. Roll it down," Sara barks on as we grab the ribs inside the boat and rotate it 180 degrees.

"Now, slowly lower the boat into the water." As we settle the boat into the water, the bow slips from my wet hands and strikes the dock with a loud crack. Mike, who is watching the launch from the other end of the dock, gives me the same disapproving look I got when I fouled Sara in the barge. If I were a real student, he probably would have chewed me out. But he is being respectful, and, frankly, I'm not altogether sad about this.

After shoving my oar into the oarlock, I take off my sneakers in preparation for boarding the shell. The dock is wet, and the cold moisture penetrates my warm socks. Mike clips a tiny blinking light to the back of my Polartec jacket. This is the closest thing we have to running lights.

"On the count of three," Sara yells, "put your right foot into the boat. Now your left. Everyone sit down." We do this in unison, careful not to tip the shell, which is only twenty-one inches wide.

In front of each sliding seat is a pair of shoes permanently attached to a foot stretcher. We place our wet stocking feet into the shoes and secure them with Velcro straps.

"Hands on the dock and everyone push off," Sara says as we smoothly shove off, first with our hands and then with our oars.

The inky darkness of College Creek is punctuated only by the ghostly lights of the boathouse on the left bank and the little flashing lights clipped to each rower in the bow position of the various shells that are now idling in the water.

"Two and four, row," Sara says. The shell slowly moves forward. The crew, of course, faces the stern and, rowing backward, depends on the cox for direction.

Mr. Pickens is barely visible in a tired-looking skiff tied to the launching dock. When he pulls the starter rope, the outboard engine sputters and then roars, emitting a puff of blue smoke. Over the groaning noise, Mr. Pickens yells to the coxes.

"Row out to the Naval Academy seawall in pairs. Meet me at the flood lights." I am doing my best to recall what I learned the other day in the barge, but we are moving so slowly that it is fairly easy to row in unison.

The route to the Severn River is dotted with several bridges. The first two are hard up against each other: the King George Street Bridge, which brings traffic in and out of Annapolis, and an old railway trestle that carries a huge silver-colored heating duct into the Naval Academy. As we pass under these bridges the Naval Academy boathouse comes into view on my right. Much like the Navy team that uses this facility, the structure is neat and ample. It makes St. John's counterpart look like a rustic cottage.

Rowing now under a low-lying roadway that connects both sides of the Naval Academy, I can see to my left the imposing Nimitz Library and Alumni Hall, and to my right a mausoleum and graveyard for deceased academy graduates.

Passing under a wooden footbridge, our stroke, the experienced junior, yells a warning. "See those eight floodlights along the seawall to your right?" She is referring to several lights perched on seventy-five-foot aluminum poles that line the Naval Academy's Hospital Point playing field. "You will get to know and appreciate them very well." I'm not sure what she means, but I make a mental note.

Well into the Severn River now, I see the Chesapeake Bay off the stern, and even further in the distance, as the sun begins to rise in the east, Kent Island, which is part of the Eastern Shore. We row up the Severn and pass beneath the Naval Academy Bridge, which is an arching affair connecting Annapolis on one side of the river with the high banks of Pendennis Mount on the other. Farther up the river still, we pass under the Route 50 Bridge. Magnificent homes line the shores, teasing us with wide docks and private yachts. This is where Washington's power elite lives. For the next couple of months, this will also be our practice course. Right now I'm just enjoying the scenery.

Rowing at a steady clip, I am clearly a drag on the boat. I am gripping the oar too tightly, and as a consequence, as I go through the drive my blade sinks too deeply into the water, slowing the boat's forward momentum. I'm also having a difficult time feathering, or momentarily rotating the blade 45 degrees just as it exits the water, so that it disturbs the run of the shell as little as possible.

"Roger," the junior stroke yells at me as we make a U-turn in the river. "You're gripping the oar far too tightly and not dropping it into the water when I do. And you're not feathering correctly. Why can't you follow me like everyone else? Stop looking at the scenery and pay attention."

A few minutes later Sara, perhaps seeking revenge for the fouling episode on the barge, shrieks in her soprano voice over the mini–PA system called the cox box, "Male rower in the bow [she doesn't know my name yet], stop dragging your oar. And for heaven's sake, follow stroke. Didn't you hear what she said?"

Rowing is becoming a lesson in humility for me. Here I am, the president of a college, rowing my heart out with a boatload full of teenagers, but I'm clearly not doing very well. I lack flexibility. I don't feather my oar properly. When I'm pulling the oar toward me on the drive, I'm not getting my legs down as quickly as stroke. Most importantly, I'm no longer in control. I'm just a novice rower who doesn't know anything. Worse, my bosses are callow teenagers one-third my age. The only thing I know for certain is that, unlike Homer's submissive Greek women in the *Odyssey,* these women at St. John's are tough!

On the return trip downriver I ignore the scenery and do everything I can to focus on stroke. But I have been humiliated in front of a bunch of teenagers, and I'm not feeling very good about myself.

Once the boats have been washed down and returned to the racks, we assemble in a little yard next to the boathouse to engage in calisthenics that are supposed to loosen up and relax our tired muscles. Anna, one of the team captains, leads us in a series of twists and bends. My back is so stiff from our brief row up the river and back that I can barely get my hands below my kneecaps. Anna, on the other hand, is a contortionist who not only can touch her toes but can also pull her legs up and around her neck.

After the exercises I'm still breathing hard when Anna announces that tomorrow night the team will sponsor a "Carb Party" in the new dorm, to which everyone is invited. Apparently some of the more experienced rowers will race this Saturday at Wye on the Eastern Shore, hence the need to load up on carbohydrates. I'm not sure what they mean by "carbohydrates"—beer or pasta—and I don't ask. Feeling somewhat rejected by my crew this morning, I nevertheless screw up my courage and ask Anna whether Susan and I can come as well. "Absolutely," she replies. "You're a member of the team too, Roger. We'd miss you if you *didn't* come." Her welcoming response means a great deal to me. I look forward to the party.

. . .

Since my new friends all live in campus residence halls and I live off campus, I decide that it might be fun to talk to a recent alumna of St. John's to get a more balanced perspective on student life. I invite Lisa, a 2002 graduate of the college who works for a friend of mine in Baltimore, out to lunch at a popular faculty hangout called Galway Bay. Lisa notices that some of her former tutors are in the restaurant, so once we are seated at a table in the back she talks in hushed tones, not wanting to be overheard. Because of the constant ringing I now experience in both ears, probably due to the Cisplatin I received at Johns Hopkins for my melanoma, I can hardly understand what she is saying. So I lean well over the table, sipping a Coke and nibbling on a hamburger.

Lisa tells me that she has great respect for her alma mater, especially for the faculty, but this afternoon she is on a mission. Lisa wants to share her concerns, not about student life, as I had hoped she would, but about the curriculum.

Now, I can imagine that *lots* of people might have concerns about the St. John's curriculum. It's unique. It's brash. It runs counter to all the trends in American higher education by avoiding narrow vocationalism and instead focusing on the Great Books of Western philosophy and literature. Even science and math are taught from the Great Books. Lisa says that although she enjoyed reading these books as a student, she now wonders how well St. John's graduates are prepared for the real world.

Lisa leans so close to me that we are almost nose to nose. "Homer and Plato are wonderful," she whispers, "but I question the relevancy of a curriculum that includes only a few female authors and nothing about non-Western cultures." She continues her diatribe. "Sure, the faculty frequently gets into discussions about whether or not to include these books in the program, but nothing much ever happens." She also wonders whether relying exclusively on seminars makes a lot of sense when students might benefit from an occasional lecture or a PowerPoint presentation. And what about this business of teaching across the curriculum? How much science do students *really* learn from tutors who are sometimes not scientists themselves? In short, Lisa feels that St. John's goes out of its way to avoid the real world. She notes that she is not alone among alumni in her critical appraisal.

I appreciate Lisa's heartfelt candor, but as an enthusiastic outsider who finds St. John's a breath of fresh air, I challenge some of her assumptions.

"Okay, Lisa, St. John's isn't perfect," I somewhat defensively acknowledge. "I'm not comfortable with the way science is taught either. And I really do think there could be a better representation of books authored by women, especially from the nineteenth century on. But at least the St. John's program has direction and purpose and gives the students not only an exposure to the liberal arts and sciences, but also a sense of how these major areas of human knowledge are interrelated and connected. This doesn't happen at most liberal arts colleges, where general education is often little more than a jumble of random and unconnected introductory course requirements. I wonder how prepared *their* students are for the real world."

My response to Lisa is well-meant but inadequate, because she has articulated several important and complex issues that are at the heart of an ongoing debate about not only the relevance of the liberal arts and sciences in general, but also effective methods of pedagogy and the inexorable movement toward specialization.

My own feeling is that in an era of increasing specialization and vocationalism, we still need the kind of generalists who founded our country more than two hundred years ago, people who have an appreciation for the complexities and interrelatedness of society, the courage to ask difficult and penetrating questions, and the inquisitiveness to seek intelligent and innovative answers. By allowing students to see how the principal areas of human knowledge in the natural and social sciences, in mathematics, and in the arts and humanities are related to one another, and by developing leadership skills in the environment of a residential campus, we prepare students to be our nation's leaders in business, politics and other professions.

My sense is that St. John's is doing an excellent job educating these generalist leaders, despite Lisa's opinion that it isn't. Even though the books we read in seminar are ancient, it is amazing how relevant virtually all of them are to modern society. They deal with universal and fundamental concepts of life, such as rage, death, and love, with which all of us can identify. Many of the authors we are reading were the first to write about a particular subject. Aeschylus, for instance, was among the first to envision a modern concept of justice. Herodotus was the first to write a proper history. William Harvey was the first scientist to figure out how the human circulatory system works. Newton and Leibniz invented calculus. Studying the books these great thinkers wrote long ago enables students today to think deeply about almost any topic they will encounter in their lives. Lisa is probably right that St. John's students are shortchanged by not reading more books by women or books by non-Western writers. Only so much can be accomplished in four years, however, and, in any event, I am confident that these students—all irrepressible readers—are voluntarily exposing themselves to a much larger selection of literature than what appears in the St. John's selection of Great Books.

But what of Lisa's concerns about the method of teaching at St. John's? I see both strengths and weaknesses in the seminar system. On the positive side, the seminar forces students to actually read the book under discussion, to reflect upon it and analyze it, rather than simply attend a lecture and passively take notes. But there are drawbacks to seminar, too, especially for a student like Sheldon, who suffers from being both a slow reader and extremely shy. Seminar requires students to be self-starters who can read large amounts of difficult material over a short period of time and that they are outgoing enough to actively and enthusiastically participate in the conversation. I fear that if Sheldon doesn't keep up with the reading and doesn't participate around the seminar table, his college career (at least at St. John's) will be over almost before it begins. I, too, was a slow reader when I was eighteen, and I was not very articulate. I feel almost certain that if I had entered St. John's as a freshman forty-three years ago, I also would have struggled. In sum, the seminar is a great pedagogical tool and a wonderful example of active learning, but it is not for everyone, all the time.

What intrigues me most about Lisa's lunchtime polemic is her question about whether humanists can effectively teach science and math (or the other way around). Academic overspecialization is another important issue in American higher education that St. John's has been addressing for years.

At most colleges these days, those with PhDs feel uncomfortable teaching subjects that are not in their immediate field of expertise. In fact, what they *really* want to teach is their narrow academic specialty, because that's what they feel most at ease doing. As a result, not only are students now taking an agglomeration of random and often unrelated discipline-based (as opposed to interdisciplinary) general education courses, but the courses themselves are often highly specialized classes that, far from providing a broad introduction to the liberal arts and sciences, sound suspiciously like the instructor's doctoral dissertation or master's thesis. No wonder so many college students are profoundly confused by the diffuse jumble of requirements they must satisfy. At St. John's, on the other hand, not only does the course of study have purpose and a direction, but it is further empowered by a faculty that is required to lead seminars across the Great Books and therefore across the disciplines of human knowledge. Perhaps St. John's has gone to an extreme with its de-emphasis on specialization and its elimination of majors and departments. But my own feeling is that as doctors of philosophy or masters of art or science teaching at the undergraduate level, we should be able to provide instruction in at least one discipline other than our own for the simple reason that knowledge is interrelated and interconnected.

Having eaten only a few bites of my lunch because we have been talking so long and passionately, I notice that it's almost 2 P.M. Lisa needs to get back to Baltimore and her job, so we part ways. She has gotten an important issue off her mind and seems to feel much better, but she has also clarified in my own mind the importance of the "great experiment" introduced by Stringfellow Barr and Scott Buchanan in 1937. Certainly, not every school can or should adopt the St. John's model. There are many different ways to be a liberal arts college. But I think that the spirit of the St. John's program—a connected liberal arts curriculum, a pedagogy that promotes active learning, and a faculty that is willing to cross disciplinary boundaries—is well worth being emulated by all of us.

. . .

Back at the boathouse the next morning, Mr. Pickens beckons his rowers to the erg machines for one of his early morning lectures on form. "I need a paradigmatic rower," he says, seeking a volunteer to serve as model for his demonstration.

"That's a big word, Mr. P," says Robert, a transfer from St. John's Santa Fe campus. "What does being a paradigmatic rower mean?" Robert, who sports a silver ring coiled through his lower lip, is not timorous. Neither is Mr. Pickens. He proceeds to give Robert and the rest of us a lesson on the Greek root of *paradigmatic.* He tells us that *para* means "alongside" and that *paradeigma,* from *paradeiknunai,* means "example." I wonder how many athletic directors at other schools are also etymologists.

At the end of his linguistics lesson and rowing demonstration, Mr. Pickens assigns us to boats. To my great relief, the belligerent junior stroke who yelled at me last week hasn't shown up for practice. Instead, Julie is promoted to stroke, Victoria joins the boat in the number-three position, I row at number two, and Christopher, just behind me, is assigned the bow. With the exception of Sara, we are all in the same freshman seminar.

Today's plan is to row up the Severn to the Route 50 Bridge, and then *race* back to the Naval Academy seawall. Mr. Pickens tells us that the winners will receive a tie. We are not exactly sure what receiving a tie means, but everyone is excited. We have not raced until now.

Our mighty armada of two eights (one made up of novice women and the other mixed with men and women), a varsity male quad (a coxless boat with four crew, each using two oars), and my mixed coxed four slowly moves out of College Creek. At the Naval Academy seawall we begin our row up the Severn, past the Naval Academy Bridge to the Route 50 Bridge and then a few hundred meters beyond to a green buoy on the northeast side of the river. As we all do a river turn, which requires the port side to row and the starboard side to back in the opposite direction, Mr. Pickens catches up to us in the outboard skiff.

"Now listen up," he yells through his megaphone. His booming voice is magnified by the calm waters of the river. "Because Roger is such a powerhouse, I'm going to give his boat a head start." Chuckles and guffaws are heard from the various shells. I feel mildly humiliated by this acerbic but friendly jab, but I join in the laughter as my crewmates and I get into the catch position to start our race. In the catch position, I now realize, the arms are fully extended toward the stern and the oar blade is positioned in the water toward the bow, ready to start the drive.

Mr. Pickens yells to Sara to take off. Adrenalin floods my nervous system as we glide forward at a very fast pace, faster than I have ever rowed before. I am fully aware of all my senses. I am absolutely alive. *I am racing!*

Rowing hard, I pretend that we are Odysseus's crew rowing past the various obstacles that threaten their progress. We have a slight lead over the women's novice eight and the varsity quad, but the mixed novice eight seems to have stalled far to our stern. I am wondering why this boat would quit so near the beginning of the race. "Not my problem," I think. "I better just worry about my own boat."

We continue to row hard, sometimes in unison but mostly out of concert with one another. In the heat of this first race, we have forgotten almost everything the coach has taught us.

And then disaster strikes.

As we approach the Naval Academy Bridge, I am running out of gas. Christopher and Victoria, rowing on the starboard side, are heavier than Julie and me on the port, so when they are about to pull their oars out of the water at the release, they are leaning well over the port gunwale, causing the shell to roll radically to the port side. This makes it difficult for me to pull my blade out of the water. Then, as we draw near the Naval Academy seawall and the infamous eight floodlights (which I now understand mark the terminus of the race), I catch a crab. A crab happens when a rower is unable to remove the oar blade from the water. The forward momentum of the boat then forces the oar handle up into the rower's chest or throat, sometimes with such devastating force that the rower is completely ejected from the boat. Since the oar blade now serves as a brake, the only way to recover from a crab is for the boat to stop completely.

Our boat grinds to a halt. I pull my blade out of the water and we all get back into the catch position. As we begin rowing again, the varsity quad and the women's eight, who are neck and neck with each other, sail quickly past us. We regain speed, but as we approach the finish line our boat again lists to port. Once more my blade is sucked forward and I catch a second crab as we drift over the finish line.

For some reason, perhaps because I have been imagining myself racing in one of Odysseus's *pentekonters*, a passage from
Book 12 of the *Odyssey* flashes through my mind. Rowing at
breakneck speed just after narrowly escaping the lure of the
dreaded Sirens, Odysseus's crew collectively catches a humon-
gous crab, and their boat goes dead in the water.

> We'd scarcely put that island astern when suddenly
> I saw smoke and heavy breakers, heard their booming thunder.
> The men were terrified—oar blades flew from their grip,
> clattering down to splash in the vessel's wash.
> She lay there, dead in the water . . .
>
> *(Homer* The Odyssey *12:218)*

Fortunately for Odysseus and me, we both lived to tell the
blood-curdling tale, but I feel a deep sense of embarrassment
and inadequacy. I have let my crewmates down. I begin to wonder why I am trying to compete with these teenagers. Why can't
I just admit that I no longer have the strength and stamina I did
when I was younger? Perhaps it's the nature of college presidents to feel that they must always better their peers. Perhaps
it's my type A personality. Obviously, I'm trying to prove something. But what?

We row slowly back to the boathouse. No one is talking. As we
move up College Creek, I apologize to my crewmates. "Sorry,
guys," I say. "I didn't mean to screw up so badly." Some offer a
soft, "It's okay, Roger," but I can tell they are just being kind.

Once back on terra firma I run into Mary, cox of the women's
eight. Mary is a woman in her forties whom I initially thought
was an older student, like me, until I learned that she is Mike's
wife. According to St. John's tradition, even a coach's spouse can

participate on a team. Mary tells me that there have been several crabs on the river this morning. The most serious, which immobilized the mixed eight I saw far off to our stern at the beginning of the race, involved Justin. Apparently, the crab he caught was so severe that as his oar blade was sucked down and snapped back, it dislocated his right shoulder. He was on his way to the hospital.

We all gather in the small yard where we did calisthenics the other day to find out what the awarding of ties involves. Next to Mr. Pickens is a box full of old neckties that seem to have come from the bargain bin at the Salvation Army. Some look okay, but most are god-awful. Broad ties decorated with American flags. Thin ties in gaudy pink. Green ties with large purple polka dots. The winner this morning is the varsity men's quad, which streamed past us when I caught my first crab. First the senior member of the crew and then the other three rowers receive a tie, which they proudly hold up for everyone to see.

"Okay," Mr. Pickens says, "remember to wear your ties with pride tonight at the Carb Party." As he says this, it seems that the eyes of my teammates are all glued on me. I imagine they're thinking, "You screwed up, old man. Because of you, we didn't get a tie. How did we get *you* in our boat?"

Mr. Pickens ends the ceremony by saying that tomorrow he will confer with Mike and the team captains to make next week's assignments. My bet is that I will lose my place, and maybe even be dropped from the team.

.   .   .

Before going to the Carb Party, I call Kate. I'm feeling despondent about how badly I am rowing, and especially about the two crabs I caught this morning. I'm drawn back forty-three years to a similar incident in which I didn't quite measure up to the expectations of my new classmates at Denison. It was "D-Day," a special occasion each fall when classes were unexpectedly suspended and students engaged in fun and games. The day started out bright and sunny, full of promise. Studies were difficult for me as I continued to struggle with homesickness, subpar reading and study skills, and my unconquerable shyness in class. Otherwise, I was enjoying my new life as a college man, but this was about to end.

I was running the anchor leg of a relay race for my freshman residence hall and blew a significant lead, causing my team to come in dead last. Because of me, Smith Hall didn't win a prize, and my dorm mates revealed their disappointment by giving me the cold shoulder for the rest of the week. It seemed that I couldn't do anything right, inside or outside the classroom, and my insecurity caused me to sink further into a funk.

Kate listens patiently to my tale of woe. About the two crabs I caught this morning. About my humiliation at the hands of Sara and the junior stroke the day before. About my frustration with not being in control.

"Dad, get over it," she says. "Every rower catches a crab at some point. And it's not all your fault. If the boat was listing to port, it obviously wasn't balanced. Everyone is to blame." I am listening intently. "You also need to relax," she continues. She then echoes what Mr. Pickens has been trying to tell me in practice. "Stop trying to control everything. You don't always have to be boss. Just let the oar handle rest loosely in your hands and enjoy life."

Rowing is becoming a metaphor for my life. As a college

president who gives orders, fires incompetent staff, suspends problematic students, and fields phone calls from disgruntled parents, I feel a need to keep a firm grip on everything, even the oar handles. But if I just let go, if I ease up a bit, I might enjoy life more. Kate is right. I don't always have to be in control.

As Susan and I prepare to leave for the party, I remember how I handled the embarrassing gaffe at Denison when I blew the footrace. I hibernated in my dorm, afraid to face my classmates. But life has taught me never to avoid difficult situations, so we drive to campus, even though Hurricane Ivan, which devastated the panhandle of Florida last night, is slowly moving in our direction.

As I enter the residence hall common room where the Carb Party is being held, I immediately spot Justin, whose right arm is in a sling. He is talking to Michelle, stroke in his ill-fated novice mixed eight, the one that did not finish this morning's race. I walk over to Justin and express concern about his condition. He seems embarrassed that everyone is paying so much attention to him. I tell him about my double crab, which seems to make him feel a little better. Michelle then tells us about two other people who caught crabs on the river this morning. Soon we are all swapping war stories.

Over my shoulder I see Anna, our contortionist captain, in the kitchen preparing sandwiches. She rowed in the women's eight that placed second in today's race. As I just did with Kate, I share with Anna my crab story, telling her how unbalanced my boat seemed to be and also asking her for advice on how I could have better dealt with the situation. I can't quite believe that after a lifetime of giving advice to students, a student one-third my age is about to return the favor. As in seminar, where

smug

the roles of tutor and student can easily be reversed, Anna has become one of my teachers in crew.

"Roger," Anna says with the authority of a team captain, "rowing is a team effort. Everyone in the boat must do his or her part. You can have a savvy stroke or a brilliant cox, but if everyone isn't coordinated, crabs happen. You and Justin and the others need to forget about what took place this morning and do your best tomorrow. Ease up. You'll do fine. I know you will."

Out of the corner of my eye I spot Susan. Far more gregarious than I, she has been carrying on an animated conversation with some sophomores on the other side of the room. But now she is trying to get my attention. The gathering storm has intensified, and she is jabbing a finger toward the closet where I hung my raincoat. I know that she is concerned about our retriever, Angel, who is terrified of lightening and thunder and home alone in the house on Franklin Street. We leave without eating dinner, but we are happy to have made some more friends.

As we drive home, I reflect again on the *Odyssey*. Like Odysseus, I am on a perilous journey, full of formidable challenges and quixotic adventures. I remember that because of bad luck and personal folly, Odysseus not only loses his entire crew, but also barely makes it back to Ithaca in one piece. I just hope that my voyage is less eventful.

CHAPTER 4

Dysfunctional Families

Just before seminar this evening, where we will tackle Plato's *Meno,* I pop over to the bookstore to try to find a good translation of Aeschylus's *Oresteia,* the work we will be reading later this week.

The bookstore, located in the basement of Humphreys Hall, is unlike any I have ever seen. The room is dark and cool, with an arched brick wall in the back that gives one the vague feeling of being in a wine cellar. Instead of bottles of vintage wine, however, the shelves are filled with vintage books, indeed with every conceivable translation of the Great Books in the St. John's program. There are at least six translations of the *Iliad* alone! But my mission is to purchase the best translation of the *Oresteia.*

This is not as easy as you might think. A very personable-looking bookstore assistant approaches me. "How can I help you?" she asks.

Knowing nothing about translations, I ask, "What translation do you recommend for Aeschylus's *Oresteia?*"

"Well, there are several," she responds, much like my wine store manager does when I am trying to select a good chardonnay. "The Hugh Lloyd-Jones translation is very lyrical, but sometimes he uses rather heavy and archaic language. Then there is Peter Meineck's version, which is the most recent. Of course, both the Lattimore and Fagels translations are very popular."

I am overwhelmed. "But which one do *you* recommend?"

"Well, actually I like all of them," she responds.

"You have read all four translations?" I ask in disbelief.

"Yup," she responds, not blinking an eye. "Why don't you look through the translations yourself," she replies, obviously not wanting to bias my choice. "They're located right over there." She is pointing deep into the cavern, just past the brick arches.

I pull the Hugh Lloyd-Jones translation off the shelf and turn to the first page. I begin reading:

Release from this weary task of mine has been my cry unto the gods throughout my long year's watch, wherein,
couchant upon the palace roof of the Atreidae, upon my bended arm, like a hound.

(*Aeschylus* Agamemnon *1–4*)

My eyes are glazing over. This is beautiful language, but language from another era, I think to myself. I'll never make it to the end. But wait. I actually knew Hugh Lloyd-Jones in my student days. He was a visiting professor at Yale back in the late 1960s and a fellow of the residential college where I was a graduate master's assistant. Even though he was only forty-six at the time, he looked ancient to me, just as ancient as I must look to my classmates at St. John's.

Hugh Lloyd-Jones was an Oxford professor with that touch of attractive eccentricity expected of an Oxbridge don. I remember walking with him toward the college dining hall one spring evening, past a group of tourists who were inspecting a large cubist sculpture by the Sardinian-born artist Costantino Nivola. To me the sculpture looked like an amorphous bunch of concrete cubes, but when a woman with a heavy Brooklyn accent asked the tour guide what it represented, Lloyd-Jones, intending to make a joke, piped up in his well-bred Oxford accent, "It's obvious. It's a Roman orgy." The tourists were aghast, but I was amused. I never thought that almost forty years later I would meet Lloyd-Jones again, this time in the form of his authoritative translation of Aeschylus.

As much as I personally admired Professor Lloyd-Jones, however, I require something that uses more modern English, and so I pull off the shelf Robert Fagles's translation and turn to the same passage I found in Lloyd-Jones:

> Dear gods, set me free from all the pain,
> the long watch I kept, one whole year awake . . .
> propped on my arms, crouched on the roofs of Atreus
> like a dog.
>
> *(Aeschylus* Agamemnon *1–4)*

Now that's more like it. Perhaps not as poetic, but much more readable. I purchase the Fagels translation feeling that I have been very clever. I then walk over to Mellon Hall and the Monday evening seminar.

Tonight we will make a rather jarring switch from the elegant poetry of Homer to the closely argued prose of Plato in his

Meno. We have also jumped forward more than three centuries, from Greece's antediluvian past to the democratic city-states of one of the world's greatest civilizations. As if we were watching the trailers before the main feature at the movie theater, we are being given a sneak preview of the kind of material we will be reading in Plato's *Republic* near the end of the semester.

The *Meno,* written around 380 B.C.E., is a fairly straightforward fictional dialogue between Socrates, the great Athenian philosopher, and Meno, a wealthy aristocrat from Thessaly. Their conversation focuses on the teachability of virtue. As in many of Plato's Socratic dialogues, firm conclusions are never established, but along the way the reader is forced to consider some fairly heady issues.

Meno, in the beginning of his discourse with Socrates, confidently suggests that he knows what virtue is. Socrates has his doubts about this. As the dialogue between Socrates and Meno unfolds, these doubts prove to be well-founded.

Mr. Holland begins the seminar by asking about modes of enquiry in philosophical discourse: "Is the mode of enquiry in the *Meno* civil or contentious?"

" 'Contentious' is *not* how I would describe the *Meno,*" Justin suggests. "Meno himself is a very passive person."

Alyssa, a stylishly dressed woman with a rose tattoo on her right shoulder, disagrees. "Maybe Meno is passive. But Socrates is not only contentious but extremely aggressive in the way he grills poor Meno. Socrates is like my older brother. He asks me questions until I arrive at the conclusion he wants."

"But Socrates never arrives at any definite conclusion," Katrina chimes in, taking issue with Alyssa's last statement. "He is extremely frustrating." Katrina reminds me of my niece at Denison.

"What about Euclid's mode of enquiry?" someone enquires from across the table, referring to the father of geometry. "While Socrates doesn't necessarily know the answer to a philosophical problem he is proposing but instead tries to discover the answer by asking lots of questions, Euclid already knows the answer to a geometrical equation before he teaches it to his students. His mode of enquiry is radically different." She then illustrates her point by reading a selection from Euclid's *Elements*. Although referring to an outside authority is usually frowned upon at St. John's, citing Euclid is permissible since his book is being discussed in the freshman math seminars.

What I like about the drift of this seminar is that it is trying to integrate two different disciplines, philosophy and mathematics. This is important. As I tried to argue with Lisa at our Galway Bay luncheon, one of the weaknesses of the general education curricula at many liberal arts colleges is that they are often discipline-based, with random and often unconnected introductory courses. Better, in my opinion, is a liberal arts curriculum that engenders relationships. This seems to be happening in this seminar, in which students are able to see connections between different disciplines and thus (to get back to Mr. Holland's initial question) to learn different modes of enquiry and to see how they are related.

Mrs. Kronsberg deepens the conversation. "According to the *Meno,* what is the source of our knowledge about virtue?" She directs our attention to the slave boy Socrates uses to address this very issue. Through simple questioning and without suggesting the answers, Socrates appears to elicit from this uneducated boy solutions to a problem in geometry. The point Socrates makes is that knowledge of virtue is "present in those who possess it as a gift from the gods," and that therefore through a process of continuous questioning, we can eventually uncover this hidden treasure. "If the truth about reality is always in our soul," Socrates tells Meno, "the soul would be immortal so that you should always confidently try to seek out and recollect what you do not know at present" (Plato *Meno* 86b). The implication, of course, seems to be that since one's knowledge of virtue already exists in the soul, it cannot be taught.

If this is, indeed, what Socrates is saying—with Socrates one cannot always be sure—then I have a real problem. In this post-Enron world, I don't think we can assume that virtue is native to anyone's soul, especially those of our political and business leaders, who, although they are extremely intelligent and well educated, often get sucked into improprieties and scandal. I believe that to a large degree virtue is taught through exposure to one's family, to church or synagogue, and to one's teachers. What hope is there for the future of our society if we assume, as Socrates seems to, that virtue or morality cannot be taught or learned? Indeed, programs and courses in moral and ethical reasoning are needed in our colleges and universities more than ever.

By the end of the seminar I am beginning to understand Katrina's frustration. Socrates rarely answers the questions he poses, but simply asks more questions. The students around the seminar table, all children of the Information Age, want answers. What they are learning from Plato, of course, is that life doesn't always offer up clear or easy answers.

. . .

In light of my miserable performance last Friday, I am very apprehensive about this morning's practice. Apparently so is Mr. Pickens. It's not just me he is concerned about. It's all of the novices who did a lousy job last week.

"We will focus on form this morning," he tells us, "and *if* we do well, we will race again Friday." He is intimating, of course, that if we *don't* do well, we might be stuck on the erg machines forever.

A few laggards dreamily stroll into the boathouse. It's bad enough that our numbers have diminished. It only makes things worse when these guys walk in well after 6 A.M. Coach Pickens spots them like a hawk. "I want all you malefactors to wait over there," he snaps at them, pointing to the back of the boathouse.

"What does malefactor mean, Mr. P?" a kid standing next to me jokingly asks. I wonder whether there will be a repeat of last week's session on the Greek root of *paradigmatic?*

"What I mean by malefactors are those five guys over there who just walked in fifteen minutes late," Mr. Pickens says as he points his finger at the offenders. "They won't be rowing today."

The five are relegated to a corner of the boathouse like juvenile miscreants who have been given a time-out by a stern parent. While this might seem harsh, this is an important lesson. Better to learn now that if you don't show up for work, the penalty will be much more severe than not being allowed to row. More to the point, we are obviously not functioning as a team. We have yet to see that everyone suffers when even one person doesn't show up for practice or arrives late.

Because of the absences the boats have to be reconfigured

once again. I'm still rowing in a coxed four, but Christopher and Julie (who have not yet appeared) and Sara and Victoria (who have been reassigned to a women's eight) are replaced by four sophomores, one of whom is appointed cox. I am the only freshman in the boat.

The five of us pull our shell off the rack and carry it out of the boathouse and down to the dock. We don't know each other, so this ritual is done in almost complete silence. I sense an uneasy relationship between the sophomore cox and stroke. Both had been aggressively lobbying Mr. Pickens for the cox position, and the kid who was assigned stroke is not a happy camper. The stroke and cox seem extremely hostile toward each other.

As we shove off the dock our new cox issues orders. The stroke automatically countermands the orders and suggests something different. Our boat is like a dysfunctional family.

Our situation deteriorates further as we enter the Severn. There is now a lot of good-natured banter going on between the other two sophomores, Joe, who is sitting in the number-four position, and Laszlo, who sits directly in front of me.

"Your mother is a dweeb," jokes Laszlo.

"Yours is a retard," replies Joe.

They both laugh as they hurl these silly insults at each other. What amazes me is that after two weeks on the river, I blend right in. It's as though I'm invisible. And so as we row up the Severn the banter continues, some of it between the cox and stroke, who can agree on almost nothing, and some of it between Joe and Laszlo, whose mother jokes are getting extremely creative.

As we do a river turn and head back down the river at a pretty fast pace, the cox begins to chant, "This Friday, we gonna win. This Friday, we gonna win. This Friday, we gonna win," meaning that if we are still together by the end of the week, our cox expects us to win ties. The cox keeps repeating this mantra every five strokes or so: "This Friday, we gonna win." Stroke, stroke, stroke, stroke, stroke. "This Friday, we gonna win." Stroke, stroke, stroke, stroke, stroke.

Remembering back to the catastrophic racing we did last Friday, when I caught two crabs, I cringe. I'm really not up to a repeat of that bad performance, and so this "We gonna win" business has me intimidated. Just as I am having this thought, the stroke yells back at the cox, "Damn it. I don't care about winning. I didn't sign up to win. I just want to have fun. So would you please just shut the hell up?"

This comment, with which I have some sympathy, causes me to think about the place of winning in American collegiate sports and at St. John's in particular. In a way, the stroke is right. Winning should not be the only reason we row. In far too many instances, it seems like winning becomes so important that the joy of simply participating in the sport is lost. How many times have certain alumni at Randolph-Macon told me that if the college doesn't have winning teams it will lose alumni support, or media attention, or—you name it? Whether or not the students are actually enjoying themselves is rarely considered. And yet there is something to be said for winning. In life, we want to do our best and to realize our full potential. We also want to do something better than someone else. So I suppose there will always be a tension between the desire to win and simply having a good time, two concepts that don't need to be mutually exclusive, as I am discovering here at St. John's.

Our trip back to the seawall is an example of terrible rowing.

Between the "We gonna win" from the cox and the "Shut the hell up" from the stroke, we are all out of balance, and I almost catch a crab again.

I'm sure it's been said before, but rowing is like life. On some days, the sky is clear, the humidity is low, and you don't have a care in the world. On other days, the sky is cloudy, the humidity is high, and nothing seems to go right. I guess it's one of those less-than-perfect days.

My dysfunctional family drags its boat out of College Creek and walks it up to the boathouse, again in total silence. Rowing with them this morning has been an exasperating and painful experience.

I spot Sara just ahead of us yelling commands to her crew as they rack their boat. All of a sudden I begin to appreciate her. I have actually missed rowing with the freshman cox who I found so obnoxious just a few days ago. I guess she wasn't so bad after all, at least compared to what I experienced this morning.

As we are leaving the boathouse Sara gives me an approving smile. "How did things go this morning, Roger? I kind of missed yelling at you," she jokes.

I laugh and return the sentiment. "Hey, how about grabbing some coffee one of these days," I suggest spontaneously. Sara agrees, and we arrange to meet next week in the Mellon Café, a student lounge that is affectionately called "the Fishbowl."

As I am about to leave the boathouse, Mr. Pickens calls over to me, "Roger, I think we need to work on your form. I'll tell you tomorrow what I have in mind."

I'm not sure whether I should be relieved or concerned.

. . .

I decide to stake myself out in the Coffee Shop, in front of a large fireplace with Greek graffiti chalked all over its face, hoping to engage some student in conversation. It is easier than I think. No sooner do I find a seat than Shannon enters the room.

Shannon was the member of my freshman orientation tour who was curious about what a college president does. Almost six feet tall, she varies her hair color from one week to the next. Today it's a bright yellow. She is wearing a red T-shirt that shows off a good part of her midriff and a tan pair of hip-hugger jeans. She obviously wants people to see the silver ring that pierces her navel.

She spots me from the mailroom, walks over to where I am seated, and asks if she can join me. "Of course," I say, somewhat taken aback since most of the students are still somewhat wary of me. "Have a seat." As she sits down, I notice that her eyes are dilated. Is she on something?

"So what's up?" I say, trying to sound as casual as I can.

"The world sucks," she replies. "And I hate my parents."

I don't really know Shannon. I've greeted her a couple of times, mostly when we passed each other on the Quad or in the Coffee Shop, but that's about it. But I can sense that she is about to tell me her story of woe. It's amazing what teenagers will sometimes share with complete strangers.

Shannon tells me that her younger sister, someone she is obviously very close to, ran away from home last night. "Mom and Dad are always fighting. It just got too much for her," she says without much emotion. I'm not quite sure what to say, so I do my counseling bit.

"Tell me more," I whisper tentatively, not sure I want to ask the question but positive I don't want anyone in the vicinity to hear what I think she is going to tell me.

"My dad drinks too much and he is abusive," she says. "After he gets in a fight with Mom following one of his binges, he takes it out on Danielle. And I resent it. I mean, he hasn't been much better with me. Matter of fact, he has been terrible."

I get the sense that Shannon has been abused by her father, but she doesn't say any more about this.

"Anyway," she continues, "Danielle just took off. She's done this a couple of times before. I have as well. But nothing ever gets resolved. What do I do if she ends up here? I mean, I'm worrying so much about her, I can't get anything done. I'm way behind in my reading. If I get involved now, I'm out of here."

I don't know what to say. I am well aware that many students come to college with difficult family problems, including physically abusive parents or, more often, parents who are so self-absorbed that they are psychologically neglectful. Indeed, Shannon's story is sadly similar to ones I have heard at my own college.

"Have you sought counseling?" I ask. Most colleges these days have in-house therapists to help students like Shannon who are struggling with various learning disabilities, personality and eating disorders, and clinical depression, problems that didn't even have a name when I went to college forty-three years ago.

"What good can they do? They can't change anything," Shannon says as her eyes begin to water.

"Well, maybe they can't," I admit. "But obviously this whole thing has taken its toll on you. You need someone else to confide in. You can't carry the burden all by yourself."

Shannon just looks at me blankly. She is inconsolable. And I really feel for her.

"Well, thanks, Mr. Martin," she says as she gets up to leave. She has regained her composure. "Maybe you're right. But I still think the world sucks. I just don't understand why this is happening and why it has to happen to me."

"Let's stay in touch," I say with as much conviction as I can as she leaves the room. But I'm really conflicted. Even though I'm technically a student like she is, Shannon has brought out my professional instincts as a teacher and advisor. I really can feel her pain. Beyond the advice I have just given her, perhaps the best I can do right now is just to listen.

. . .

Seminar returns to Greek literature and in particular to Aeschylus (525–456 B.C.E.), the great playwright from western Attica who is the father of Greek tragedy. Aeschylus is my nemesis. Many of my classmates absolutely love the *Oresteia,* the trilogy we are now reading. The poetry is beautiful. The imagery is lush and compelling. But forty-three ago, at Denison, I got a D– on my very first writing assignment, an essay I did on the *Oresteia* for Mr. Cunningham's Western Civilization course, and I have been intimidated by Aeschylus ever since.

Actually, *Agamemnon,* the first play of the trilogy, is a wonderful companion piece to the *Odyssey* because Odysseus's joyful reunion in Ithaca with his son and wife is a stark contrast to King Agamemnon's less than happy reception by his wife Clytemnestra when he returns to Mycenae. Otherwise, both works are about blood revenge.

Agamemnon is not a nice person. Prior to leaving for the Trojan wars, he had his daughter, Iphigeneia, sacrificed to the gods. Agamemnon's enraged wife, Clytemnestra, aided by her paramour Aegisthus, schemes revenge. Almost as soon as Agamemnon lands in Argos with his slave and concubine Cassandra (daughter of King Priam and sister to Hector and Paris), both are murdered. But Agamemnon's death is just the prelude to more mayhem and bloodletting.

In *The Libation Bearers,* the second play of the trilogy, Agamemnon's son and daughter, Orestes and Electra, seek revenge for their father's murder, and both Clytemnestra and Aegisthus die at the hands of Orestes. The dual themes of rage and honor, so prevalent in both the *Iliad* and the *Odyssey,* are continued by Aeschylus. But the more modern themes of justice and reconciliation are the focus of the *Eumenides,* the third and final play, as these dastardly deeds are sorted out and made sense of by, among others, Athena, the goddess of wisdom.

My problem with Aeschylus is that I think like a historian rather than like a poet. Not quite understanding that Homer and Aeschylus are writing fiction, I read *Agamemnon* as history. Perhaps this is why I got the D– in Mr. Cunningham's Western Civ class. I am particularly drawn to the beginning of this play, in which the tragic aftermath of the Trojan War is translated into terms that anyone who has been through such a conflict can understand. The chorus describes the feelings of the bereaved families when their loved ones arrive home in large urns, the ancient equivalent of modern body bags, and raises again the interesting question, posed at seminar several weeks ago, whether Homer and now Aeschylus are writing antiwar poems:

> They knew the men they sent,
> but now in place of men
> ashes and urns come back
> to every hearth.

War, War, the great gold-broker of corpses
holds the balance of the battle on his spear!
Home from the pyres he sends them,
   home from Troy or the loved ones,
heavy with tears, the urns brimmed full,
   the heroes return in gold-dust,
dear, light ash for men; and they weep,
They praise them, 'He had skill in the swordplay,'
    'He went down so tall in the onslaught,'
'All for another's woman.' So they mutter
in secret and the rancor steals
towards our staunch defenders, Atreus' sons.
                (Aeschylus Agamemnon *431–46,*
                      trans. Fagles)

I read these words just after watching the evening news and more disturbing reports of American and Iraqi dead in another Baghdad massacre, and I feel great sadness. But this is tragic poetry, not tragic history, and I sense that if connections to the *Oresteia* are to be made in seminar, they will be of a literary variety rather than in the form of commentary on contemporary events.

I enter Mellon 101 a few minutes early and find a small group of students at the end of the table listening to Seth, the kid with the Amish-style beard. Well known for his humorous one-liners and quips during class, Seth is wondering out loud whether he has missed something in his reading of Aeschylus. "Isn't the *Oresteia* a slam dunk?" he asks rhetorically. "I mean, Clytemnestra kills her husband and then she gets killed in return by her son. Why do we have to spend two hours discussing this?" But before Seth's question can be answered, more students and then the tutors arrive and seat themselves around the table.

I notice with concern that most of my classmates have bought the Lloyd-Jones translation of the *Oresteia*. So have Mr. Holland and Mrs. Kronsberg. I thought I was being clever by purchasing the easier-to-read translation by Fagles. Not only am I now feeling *really* disloyal to a scholar I very much admired in my youth (I wonder whether his translation is perhaps the better one), but I am also having a difficult time following the conversation since the translation they are using is so different from mine.

The *Oresteia* is far from a slam dunk. Once Mrs. Kronsberg asks the opening question, the nonstop discussion covers a wide range of issues. Why did Agamemnon kill his daughter Iphigeneia? How justified was Clytemnestra in killing Agamemnon and especially Cassandra, who, after all, was somewhat innocent in this sordid affair? Was it the Furies, the ancient goddesses of vengeance, who caused all this to happen? There is very little consensus about these matters.

Mr. Holland picks up on the vengeance theme, which leads to a discussion of Clytemnestra's motive for killing Agamemnon. Does she kill him as revenge for the death of Iphigeneia? Or does she do it because she has a lust for power and wants to rule Agamemnon's kingdom herself?

There is agreement around the table that Agamemnon's household represents a dysfunctional family at its worst. Not only do husband and wife cheat on each other—Agamemnon with Cassandra and Clytemnestra with Aegisthus—but the entire plot revolves around an instance of severe parental abuse, namely, Agamemnon's complicity in his daughter's death. For this act, his wife is understandably furious. During Agamemnon's long absence her anger slowly builds into a withering rage. You can sense that there is no love lost when, immediately after murdering her husband, Clytemnestra obsesses with the chorus:

> I brooded on this trial, this ancient blood feud
> year by year. At last my hour came.
> Here I stand and here I struck
> and here my work is done.
> I did it all. I don't deny it, no.
> He had no way to flee or fight his destiny
> . . .
> Rejoice if you can rejoice—I glory.
> And if I'd pour upon his body the libation
> it deserves, what wine could match my words?
> It is right and more than right. He flooded
> the vessel of our proud house with misery,
> with the vintage of a curse and now
> he drains the dregs. My lord is home at last.
>
> *(Aeschylus* Agamemnon *1396–1401/1417–23,*
> *trans. Fagles)*

It then dawns on me that this poem is also about family relations. I immediately think of Shannon and her dilemma. Mother and father fighting. Abusive parents. Rage. How will that situation end in her case? Hopefully not in violence. But who knows? I just wonder how Shannon is dealing with *Agamemnon* in her seminar, just down the hall from where I am sitting.

It's 10:15 P.M. and impatient Seth says, quite audibly, "Let's end." From across the table, Mrs. Kronsberg gives him the evil eye. She is using nonverbal language to tell Seth that the tutors, not students, end seminar.

.   .   .

I make a rookie mistake as a journalist and pay for it. Until now I have been mostly invisible at crew. As was apparent the other day, students will say things in my presence that they would *never* say in the presence of their parents or another adult. This anonymity has provided me with a golden opportunity to capture some very candid student assessments of St. John's and college life in general. But yesterday, in a private conversation with Mr. Pickens following practice, I joked about the colorful language I hear in my boat. This morning, Laszlo, one of yesterday's vocal sophomores, approaches me at the door of the boathouse looking quite somber and contrite.

Laszlo is obviously very popular with his crewmates. As he walks toward me, he is greeted by his buddies with "Hey Laz Lo," followed by high fives and knowing winks. However, once we are alone in the silent company of the erg machines near the front of the boathouse, he says in hushed tones, "Mr. Martin, I need to apologize to you. I feel so badly." The pained expression on his face makes him look as if he did something terrible.

"Apologize for what?" I ask, genuinely puzzled.

"You know, the bad language in the boat yesterday."

It then dawns on me that after receiving my report on the chatter in my boat, Mr. Pickens probably told Laszlo and Joe to keep their mouths shut when rowing and to apologize to me for the colorful language.

I tell Laszlo not to worry and that I really wasn't offended. But no sooner do I finish saying this than Coach Pickens begins one of his early morning orations.

"Okay everyone, listen up." As he says this, the coach is looking directly at Laszlo. "From now on there will be no more talking in the boats. Am I making myself crystal clear?" As he asks this question, I feel as though everyone's eyes are on me. "If you are talking," Coach concludes, "you aren't concentrating. And when you aren't concentrating, you're not rowing properly. Okay. Now get your boats. The women's eight first."

I cringe at the idea that my conversation with Mr. Pickens is well known to the entire boathouse and that they might now see me as a snitch, an interloper, around whom only civil language will be tolerated. Again, I realize that as much as I want to be a freshman like the others, I'm still a college president, and the coach will not tolerate bad behavior in front of such a distinguished guest. Then again, maybe none of this happened. Maybe Laszlo actually felt guilty about what he considered to be a terrible indiscretion. I'll never know. Paranoia and self-doubt have again overtaken me; paranoia because I fear that the students in my boat might see me not as a fellow student, but as some kind of antique curiosity, self-doubt because the insecurities of my real freshman year so long ago continue to haunt me.

On the other hand, Mr. Pickens gives me a gift this morning. Yesterday he suggested that he had a plan for how I could improve my form. This morning he tells me exactly what he has in mind. I am to scull in a double with Tom, one of the team's captains. Sculling in a double involves each person rowing with two oars like you do in a rowboat.

Tom and I scull together on College Creek and I pick up a few helpful pointers from him. He shows me how better to feather my oars, how to move more slowly up the slide, and then how to accelerate into the release.

After we have rowed up and down College Creek a few times and have settled into a comfortable pace, I ask Tom to tell me a little about himself. Like many Johnnies I have met, Tom has had a love-hate relationship with education. He tells me that he did not feel challenged in high school, where he was bored most of the time. So, instead of going to college right away, he joined the National Civilian Community Corps, where he did community service for a couple of years and also read lots of fiction. When his time with the NCCC was over, Tom applied to only one college, St. John's, because of its unique curriculum that stressed reading. He says he has not regretted the decision.

As we row back down College Creek toward the boathouse, I make an innocent observation: "Like you, Tom, so many of the freshmen I have met applied only to St. John's. They seem to have a real sense of what it means to be a Johnnie even before they get here."

"Maybe so," Tom responds as we approach the dock. "But they aren't Johnnies when they arrive."

"So when does that happen?" I ask, surprised by his response.

"When they have completed Plato's *Republic.* Then they become Johnnies."

Like many of his classmates, Tom views his college in the context of the Great Books. Bragging rights at most colleges begin the moment a student is accepted, or at least by the time they have matriculated. But at St. John's, the curriculum defines when you actually become a member of the community.

After Tom and I store our boat and I am about to leave the boathouse, Mary approaches me and says that she and Mike, the assistant coach, would like to have Susan and me over to their house for dinner. Mary has been very supportive of my rowing efforts, and we have become friends. But I'm not sure whether

P₁tA

it's good form for a freshman like me to socialize with a coach and his wife. Roles can get confused. And yet there is part of me that welcomes some interaction with older adults, and so I gladly accept.

. . .

I walk to my scheduled meeting with Sara in the Mellon Café. Unlike the subterranean Coffee Shop in McDowell, Mellon Café is a starkly modern affair enclosed on both sides by tall glass walls that reach from the room's blond wood floor to its cherrywood ceiling. On the opposite side, framed by a large picture window, is a courtyard with trees and shrubbery. Since you can't really buy coffee here, the students have appropriately renamed this room "the Fishbowl," which is exactly what it resembles. At the moment the room is empty except for Sara, who is sitting alone at a table next to the window overlooking the courtyard and is reading the *Oresteia*. She affectionately waves as I approach her table.

"How do you like the *Oresteia*?" I ask her as I pull up a seat.

"It's my favorite," she replies. It seems to me that whenever I ask students at St. John's what their favorite book is, it's almost always the one they are currently reading.

I sit down facing Sara. She seems far less threatening sitting across the table from me than she does in the stern of our boat. And she seems like a *really* nice person, not the ogre I had sized her up to be when we first rowed together.

Sara tells me that she attended Northgate High School, just outside of Pittsburgh, where she was valedictorian. I can tell she is very bright—and sociable as well. As in our boat, she exudes considerable confidence even in the presence of an older person, something that does not come naturally to most college freshmen.

I ask Sara how she learned about St. John's.

"I read about the college in *Smithsonian* magazine," she says, "and just fell in love with the idea of attending a college that featured the Great Books." She tells me that she enjoys St. John's immensely. "It's even better than I hoped," she says.

We joke about our first encounter in the barge, when neither of us had a clue how to row. She apologizes for yelling at me the first day she coxed our four and admits that it was disconcerting blaring at someone who reminded her of her father.

"Okay, Sara," I say, feeling quite comfortable talking to this eighteen-year-old. "Now fess up. You coxed before, didn't you? I mean, you seem really professional out there on the river."

"Not really," she says. "Until I came to St. John's I didn't do sports. I mean, just look at me. Do I look like a jock?" Before I can respond, she continues, "One of the reasons I chose St. John's is because I wanted to experience being an athlete, and I knew that I probably wouldn't be able to do that at most colleges. Certainly not crew."

I reflect on what Sara has just said. The athletic program at St. John's is especially designed for students like her—and me, for that matter—who either were not athletes in high school or want to try out an entirely different sport in college. To me, this philosophy of athletics seems in keeping with the liberal arts mission, which should be to encourage students to experiment both academically and in their extracurricular activities. Sadly, this is not the case at far too many colleges and universities these days. Student athletes are not only heavily recruited, but recruited to be fullbacks or point guards or goalies. Walk-ons—unrecruited students who just show up at practice—are a vanishing breed. Moreover, student athletes who want to try out something new, like editing the school newspaper or working as a lab assistant, find it difficult to schedule these activities because playing seasons and practice times are expanding exponentially. Bottom line, college students should have the opportunity to participate in a variety of sports as well as engage in nonathletic activities.

I ask Sara what she plans to do when she graduates four years from now. "Go into some kind of church work," she tells me without missing a beat. Sara knows exactly what she wants to do with her life, which is unusual for an eighteen-year-old.

We talk like this for over an hour, just two classmates shooting the breeze. Before we leave, however, Sara asks me a question.

"Roger," she says, "you never learned how to do the waltz or swing dance, did you?" Sara obviously spotted me at the waltz lessons during orientation.

"Guess not," I say. "Never could dance very well."

"No excuses," she responds. "If you can learn how to row, you can learn how to dance. See you at the next Waltz Party."

I begin to worry again.

.   .   .

What a difference a week makes. This morning almost the entire crew will compete in a tie race, and I am selected to row in a mixed eight. Half the crew are men and half women. Tom, my instructor from yesterday, will be the cox, and Anna, another captain, the stroke. I figure that Mr. Pickens has selected the worst rowers on the team for this boat so that we can learn from two of the best. Christopher is also assigned to my shell, as is Victoria.

Remembering last week's events, I am concerned about my

stamina, especially when, as we shove off the dock in the morning darkness, Coach Pickens announces from his skiff that we will row at a fairly brisk pace up the Severn River to the Route 50 Bridge, execute a river turn, and then immediately do a "power race" all the way back to the Naval Academy seawall, some 2,700 meters in all. "Power race" sounds alarmingly ominous to me. But the shell I am in seems to be well balanced, and as we row out of College Creek and up the Severn River, I am doing fairly well.

This early in the morning there is very little traffic on the Severn. The only other people on the river are watermen checking their crab traps. Their vessels vary from thirty to sixty or seventy feet in length, and when they quickly move from buoy to buoy to pull up their traps, they cause wakes that can swamp a narrow shell. When these crab boats steam past us, we have to slow down and then lay our oar blades flat on the turbulent water to stabilize our shells.

This morning, however, there is another problem. As one of these trawlers passes us to the port, I hear catcalls from two rather scruffy-looking watermen—"Hooah, hooah!"—while they make obscene gestures with their left forearms. This boorish behavior is not typical of most watermen, who are usually very courteous, but I am again reminded how vulnerable female college students can be to the unwanted advances of the male species, especially older men who should know better. This time, however, I feel personally involved, as though these insults were being hurled at my two daughters. But what can I do? Tell them that they better watch out because I'm an important college president? So I just suck wind. We finally reach the starting point of our race, a few meters short of the Route 50 Bridge.

This time my boat is not the first to leave. The all-women eight to our starboard starts off down the river thirty seconds ahead of us. We are next to go, followed by the two all-male eights with experienced crews.

We are clipping along at a fairly brisk pace. Anna performs excellently at stroke and is an inspiration to all of us. Tom is trying to get us pumped up by yelling that we are gaining on the women. We all row harder as we approach Horseshoe Point, just above the Naval Academy Bridge. I'm focused on Anna's oarlock so that my blade is entering the water just when hers is. I am no longer appreciating the scenery as I did the first day I rowed on the river. I'm also remembering what Kate told me, and I'm relaxing, not gripping the oar handle so tightly, letting my blade just fall into the water, and initiating the drive with my legs rather than with my arms.

We are now under the Naval Academy Bridge and I am beginning to feel pain—all over, but especially in my hands, lower arms, and back—and I'm struggling to stay focused. I pray, "Lord, don't let me catch a crab," as we approach the first of eight floodlights along the Naval Academy seawall. I know that there are only five hundred meters to go, so I pull hard, still focusing on Anna's oar blade.

We're now in first place, having passed the women's eight. The two men's eights, however, are gaining on us. Then, at the fourth floodlight, Victoria's seat runs off its track and we completely lose momentum. After all that effort, we come in dead last. I am just thankful that I wasn't the problem this time. But I also feel badly for poor Victoria, who, I'm sure, is experiencing the same discouragement I did when I caught my two crabs several weeks ago. I commiserate with Victoria and tell her that it happens to everyone.

As we enter College Creek and approach the King George Street Bridge, everyone looks up and waves at an older woman who waves at us in return. It is Eva Brann, the seventy-five-year-old St. John's tutor who Don pointed out to us during our orientation tour. Later this morning I will have coffee with her. This is indeed a close-knit community, and I feel very fortunate to be part of it.

After unloading and racking our boats, we reassemble next to the boathouse. Mr. Pickens gives out ties to each member of the winning men's eight. He also tells us that in anticipation of two major races later in the season, the Severn Chase against the Annapolis Rowing Club and the intercollegiate Head of the Occoquan in northern Virginia, practice from now on will take place five days a week, Tuesday through Saturday, instead of just four. We collectively groan. The coach then tells us that he wants those who plan to participate in these races to make a solemn commitment to show up *every* morning at 6 A.M. sharp. Those who don't want to make this commitment can row at their own leisure in single sculls.

I want to make the commitment. I desperately want to race at Occoquan.

· · ·

"So we are already on a first-name basis," Miss Brann says as I enter her house on Wagner Street, hard up against the Naval Academy. This is a private joke between us. Until a week or so ago I avoided consorting with faculty other than my tutors because I wanted to maintain my appearance as a student. But Eva Brann is a St. John's luminary, and when Don told my tour group that "The St. John's experience isn't complete until you've had her in seminar," I knew right then that I had to meet her.

Then one day, I ran into her outside the Coffee Shop. On that occasion I followed St. John's protocol and addressed her as "Miss Brann." I told her what I was doing at St. John's, and we agreed to meet. But when I called yesterday to confirm our meeting, I inadvertently slipped into my presidential role and addressed her as "Eva." I should have been more sensitive to the fact that this seventy-five-year-old scholar is a person of gravitas, and civility is still important to her.

"I'm sorry," I say, feeling embarrassed. "It's just that since I turned sixty last year I tend to address my peers on a first-name basis. I guess I was being presumptuous."

"You're not *sixty,* are you?" she asks in amazement. "You look much, much younger. But please come in. Come in." The ice has been broken.

Miss Brann lives in part of a modest two-family wood-frame house that seems out of scale with the enormous campus of the Naval Academy, which can be seen just over a wall from her street. We walk through her living room and into the kitchen, where she has neatly set up a tea service. The living room is filled with antiques and memorabilia and has the musty but pleasant smell of a house that has been lived in by the same person for many years.

Miss Brann, an archaeologist by training with a PhD from Yale, has been at St. John's for forty-seven years. Forty-seven years! I don't know anyone who has been teaching at the same institution for that long. I take a few sips of tea and then ask her a question that has been on my mind since I arrived at the college. "You probably know more about these things than anyone on the faculty," I say. "In your opinion, what constitutes a 'Great Book'?"

"Well, I'm not sure about knowing more than my colleagues," she responds modestly, "but in my mind great literature is something that is not only beautiful, but of perennial value."

I agree with her. I tell her that I am finding the ancient books I am reading in freshman seminar not only beautiful to read, but also very modern, as they speak to my own condition.

"What changes have you witnessed at St. John's during your long tenure?" I ask, thinking that the college must have undergone tremendous transformation over the almost fifty years she has been a tutor here.

"Really very little," she responds. "If anything, the faculty is stronger than when I arrived here in the mid-1950s."

"Do they get along with each other?" I ask.

"Yes, they do. They really do." She pauses. "Of course, when they discuss changing the program, the conversation can get quite heated." I think back to my meeting with Lisa at Galway Bay and I understand what Miss Brann means.

Thinking about Lisa encourages me to ask another question that has been perplexing me. "Does this teaching across the curriculum business really work? I mean, how do you, as a humanist, feel leading a science lab?"

"I think it works reasonably well," she responds. "At St. John's the science and math labs deal with fundamental principles that any educated person should be able to understand."

She then tells me something I didn't know before, that there are weekly meetings for faculty leading seminars and labs to compare notes and ask questions of knowledgeable colleagues. "So if you are newly leading a freshman science lab on, say, Lavoisier's *Elements of Chemistry*," she says, "and you don't quite understand his analysis of atmospheric air, you have an opportunity to meet with fellow tutors also leading the science lab who are experienced with the material. They can answer your questions." "Most importantly," she quickly adds so I don't miss her point, "by leading seminars and labs across the Great Books, and teaching tutorials in the various liberal arts, the tutors are permitted to become learners themselves. It really is a great joy."

I am sympathetic. I have long felt that one of the virtues of a small liberal arts college is that it affords people like me an opportunity to meet scholars outside their academic discipline and to learn from them. St. John's just does this in a more deliberate and focused way than most.

"What about the students?" I ask, changing the subject. "How have they changed?"

"Oh yes, the students." As she says this, her eyes begin to sparkle. "When I began my career here, the students of the 1950s and '60s were a wonderful group, no doubt about it. But the students today? They are exceptional. They are inquisitive. They enjoy reading. And they are responsive." She tells me that when there is a problem student in a seminar—someone who dominates the conversation, for instance—the students themselves will often talk to the offender after class. She feels that this indicates not only that the students are invested in the seminar, but also that they are taking on responsibility and leadership.

"Wow," I think to myself. "What an endorsement for the future leaders of our country."

. . .

I get to seminar early. Seated in the room alone is Zach, who is reading this evening's assignment. Zach is a big roly-poly kind of guy. He has thick black hair, usually uncombed, and when someone sneezes in seminar, he almost always says, very loudly, "God bless you." He gives me a big greeting.

I sit next to him and we shoot the breeze. Zach comes from Owings, Maryland, where he lived with his mother and father, his younger brother, and his grandmother. His dad works for the Pentagon, and his younger brother attends college in Florida. Like many St. John's students, Zach was homeschooled by his mother. He obviously comes from a close family.

Zach tells me that he has always loved the classics, so he knew early on that he would attend St. John's. Indeed, like Tom, he applied nowhere else. Between karate, his great passion, and the Japanese Animation Club, which he has just joined, Zach seems to be enjoying college life.

We are oblivious to the fact that other students have entered the room and have seated themselves around the table. Indeed, we are so engrossed in conversation that we fail to notice that Mrs. Kronsberg and Mr. Holland have arrived. I eventually look across the table and notice that both of them and the rest of the class are patiently waiting for Zach and me to be silent. Zach's face turns red with embarrassment.

Most of this evening's seminar focuses on the *Eumenides,* the third play in Aeschylus's trilogy, in which Orestes is brought to trial for killing his mother. The god Apollo champions Orestes' cause, but the Furies, ancient goddesses themselves, are extremely angry with Orestes for what he did to his mother and would like to string him up on the nearest olive tree. In many ways, Orestes' trial is a triumph over this kind of frontier justice.

Mrs. Kronsberg asks why Apollo petitions Athena to adjudicate the bitter conflict. Jessie, who often sits with her feet folded up underneath her on the chair, suggests that while Apollo has championed Orestes' cause, Athena has not been party to the conflict and therefore is in a better position to render an impartial judgment. Nathaniel agrees, adding that Athena is the goddess of wisdom and therefore the most likely to be unbiased in the case before her.

Mr. Holland asks, "Now, what are we saying the defining feature of Athena's wisdom is?"

"Fairness," Alyssa quickly responds, suggesting that Athena has a balanced view of the conflict, whereas the Furies clearly have it in for Orestes. Morgan finds it interesting that the Furies don't go after Aegisthus, who, after all, was an accessory to the murder of Agamemnon. He suggests that this might be because under the old system of Greek justice represented by the Furies, blood relationships are paramount, and Aegisthus is neither a husband nor a brother.

Conversation about old versus new traditions of justice continue apace. As this happens, I begin to see the connection between the books we read at the beginning of the seminar—the *Iliad* and the *Odyssey*—and what will come later, such as Plato's *Republic*. In Homer's ancient Greece, justice is violent and based largely on blood relationships and family feuds. Thus, when Paris, a Trojan, absconds with Helen, the wife of

Menelaus and a Greek, Agamemnon leads a flotilla of Greek ships to seek revenge for his brother's humiliation. The result is the wholesale slaughter of thousands of people on both sides of the conflict and the eventual destruction of Troy. Two hundred years later, we see in Aeschylus the emergence of a new tradition, one in which justice is no longer controlled by the gods and in which blood relationships and personal feuds count less than law and order, a tradition that will be perfected by Plato in the *Republic*. In time, and incorporating ideas from both the Enlightenment and Christianity, the Founding Fathers of our country will develop this concept of justice even further, resulting in the creation of the Declaration of Independence and the United States Constitution, documents that will be studied and read by these students in their junior year.

Tim sums things up perfectly: "Athena represents the new order in Greek society, defined by law and order. The Furies represent the old, defined by chaos and vengeance. But Athena knows that you can't eliminate the old system overnight. And so she must reason with the Furies, and make them feel part of the new system that is being introduced."

The seminar ends with an observation made by Alyssa about how surreal the conversion of the Furies to the rule of law is. Throughout the trilogy, the Furies are passionate for revenge. Then, boom, they are converted by Athena to follow a more rational and just system for adjudicating wrong deeds. "Maybe they are intimidated," Alyssa jokes. "After all, Athena has access to Zeus's thunder bolts."

"Right," says Jessie. "They are given a deal they can't refuse. They see the writing on the wall."

What I like about this evening's conversation is that, unlike our first meeting back in August, when everyone deferred to the two tutors and a few male students dominated the conversation, now the students—both men and women—are conversing with one another. The tutors are still asking the opening questions, but their role in seminar has become almost secondary. Seminar has taken on a life of its own.

. . .

It's a beautiful fall afternoon, almost an Indian summer, and I am sitting on a bench outside the Quad under the shadow of a large oak. I am trying to get a head start on Plato's *Gorgias,* the next work we will be reading in seminar. But the day is too beautiful to be reading, and I'm just watching the students come and go from the Coffee Shop.

I am becoming a fixture at St. John's. Students no longer look at me as though I were some kind of freak who doesn't belong in their midst. Instead I am often greeted with a smile or a hello. Students will also walk up to me to talk, like Shannon recently did.

Sheldon ascends the steps to the Quad, spots me, and strolls over. I think I am becoming his father confessor.

"Hey. What's up?" I greet him. As usual, he looks hassled as he sits next to me on the bench.

"It's Mom again," he responds rather glumly as he sits beside me. "I should never have told her about John." John is Sheldon's roommate from Philadelphia's Main Line.

"What did you tell her?" I ask.

"Oh, about how he makes me really angry when he is with his girlfriend and wants me to leave the room so that he can do . . . you know what?"

"No, what?" I ask, being rather dense.

"You know, he does *it* with her. In my room. Can you believe?"

"Okay," I say apologetically. "*Now* I think I understand."

"Well," he continues, "I think Mom has called Ms. Seeger to complain and demand that I get a new roommate. At least that's what she said she was going to do. But it's so embarrassing. I mean, what do I do if it gets out that my roommate is doing *it* with his girlfriend in our room?"

"That's not good," I say, thinking how naïve Sheldon is not to see that, in the eyes of his classmates, his mother's behavior is just as mortifying as his roommate's. But before I can further discuss this matter with him, Sheldon is off on another problem.

"And if that weren't enough to deal with, my mother wants me to drop Melee."

"Why?" I ask.

"She says it's a silly activity that I'll never be able to put on my resume."

Sheldon's mother is the classic "helicopter parent" that I see with regularity on my own campus, constantly hovering over her child to make sure that nothing goes wrong, but assuring in the process that it probably will. Helicopter parents are an interesting phenomenon. Like many from the baby boomer generation, they tend to be overly protective of their Millennial children. I don't know why, but perhaps they are trying to compensate for the latchkey parents many of them had when they were children. They are also extremely demanding and aggressive. Largely because tuitions are so expensive, these parents feel that college is a commodity, much like a new automobile. If the engine is stalling, don't bother with the salesperson who sold you the car. Take your complaints directly to the CEO of General Motors.

The problem, of course, is that college is supposed to be a place where students transform from adolescents to adults; it is where, in addition to receiving a good education, they learn how to become independent human beings and good citizens. When parents continue to relate to their children as though they never left home, when they are constantly calling their children on the phone or frequently visiting them on campus, this maturing process is severely compromised. Parents need to love and support their children, but at the same time let them deal with life. Sometimes that means letting them make mistakes.

This conversation with Sheldon and the one I had earlier with Shannon causes me to think of both of them against the backdrop of Aeschylus. Like Orestes and his sister Electra, both of my friends belong to troubled families. In Shannon's case, a young woman and her sister are rebelling against their uncaring parents. In Sheldon's, a young man is being smothered by his hovering mother. Both students are in bad situations, but their troubles are nothing compared to those of Orestes and Electra, who are so conflicted by their mother's behavior that they kill her. Nothing is quite so messy as Greek tragedy.

· · ·

Big disappointment. Although after Mr. Pickens's talk at the last practice I decided to make the commitment to compete in the races later this season, I discover that I have been relegated to sculling practice, or what in the boathouse is derisively called "skulking camp." Almost everyone else is assigned a racing eight or four.

I'm heartbroken. No, I am feeling the rage of Achilles! Contact with students is the real reason I went out for crew in the first place. Rowing in a single scull, though, is a solitary activity. I'm not getting up at 5 A.M. five mornings a week to row by myself on College Creek. Second, I really *do* want to race with other students, like my daughter did when she went to college. I know I'm being childish, but I have become obsessed with the idea of racing in an eight-man shell at Occoquan.

Mike is assigned the responsibility of supervising skulking camp. I approach him off to one side of the boathouse and tell him that sculling by myself is not why I am here. Poor guy. He can tell that I am really angry, but there is little he can do about it. Mike suggests I talk to Mr. Pickens, who is on the other side of the boathouse trying to get the larger boats launched. I walk over to him.

"Coach," I say, almost with a pout, "why don't I just stay back this morning and observe? Or maybe go out on the skiff with you? I *really* don't want to scull all by myself." I am hoping he can see the disappointment in my face.

"Roger, this is neither the time nor the place. Just work with Mike, will you?" he answers rather curtly before he returns to what he was doing before I interrupted him.

I realize that I shouldn't burden him with my little problems, but on the other hand I'm *really* angry, so I impulsively decide to leave the boathouse. I'm having a full-blown hissy fit, just like Achilles did when he didn't get his way with Agamemnon and abruptly left the battlefield. I storm out of the back door, stomp up the wooden steps, and march off toward the parking lot.

But when I'm halfway to my car, I stop. I suddenly realize that I'm being an absolute idiot. This is what I did when I was a freshman at Denison forty-three years ago. I quit when things were not going well. But now I'm a sixty-one-year-old college president, and college presidents don't deal with adversity by having a tantrum, especially over a minor setback like being required to row in a single scull. I do an about-face.

And it's a good thing I make this decision, because when I return, looking somewhat sheepish about leaving in the first place, Coach Pickens, who has apparently had a change of heart as well, assigns me to a double with Jackie, a senior I haven't seen around the boathouse until recently. I am now as happy as a clam. I can row. And I can row with a student. Life is sweet.

The remnants of a rather violent storm are passing over Annapolis, and the Severn River is too choppy to row on. So everyone, including the eights, fours, doubles, and single sculls, stay on College Creek, creating an enormous traffic jam.

Jackie and I row over to an estuary on the northern side of the creek along with two other doubles and a handful of single sculls. We catch up to Mike, who is himself rowing in a single scull, and practice our form under his supervision. We must look like a flock of ducklings being carefully watched by their mother.

Jackie, who sits in the stern of our boat, acts as a combined stroke and cox and is therefore in a position to give orders. "I hope I'm not being too bossy," she apologizes as she instructs me to pull harder on my starboard oar. "I've never been in a position to tell guys what to do," she confesses. I can tell Jackie is secretly enjoying her newfound power, a power I hope she will continue to cultivate. When Jackie goes out into the real world she will almost certainly have to supervise men as well as women. I am enjoying myself as well, thankful that I didn't get stuck alone in a single scull.

Jackie, who is very pleasant, tells me that she joined crew only yesterday, and so I ask her why she decided at the last minute to do this crazy sport. She tells me that some of her friends are on the team and they encouraged her to join them. And, of course, in the St. John's tradition, she is welcomed even though she is starting late. The St. John's motto is "Never too late to start something new." Between strokes I ask Jackie what she plans to do after graduation.

"I'm not sure," she says. "Maybe travel around Europe. Maybe live in Cambridge." Jackie reminds me of so many seniors who don't have a clue what they want to do after receiving their sheepskin and all too often end up continuing to be a financial burden on their parents.

Jackie and I chat like this for at least an hour before we finally return to the boathouse. As we do this, I count my blessings that I didn't prematurely end my rowing career at St. John's.

CHAPTER 5

Navy

Whenever I speak at college admission events, foremost on the minds of parents is whether a liberal arts and sciences education is worth the expensive tuition they must pay. "Wouldn't my kid be better off taking vocational courses that actually prepare her to do something?" are words that are very familiar to me. Many of these parents think that the primary purpose of a college education is to prepare their children for a high-paying first job. Consequently, they have a difficult time understanding why, for example, philosophy or a foreign language is required for graduation.

There is a good reason why a liberal arts and science education makes sense in the brave new world our children will face. While my father's generation of college graduates could feel secure knowing they would be employed by Chrysler or Xerox forever, rapid changes in our society, brought on in large part by massive advances in technology, have altered this situation rather dramatically. The current generation of students will have not just one career, but as many as seven or eight completely different ones before they retire. And in my opinion, the best preparation for the very fluid and ever-changing world we live in, at least for those aspiring to positions of leadership, is *not* narrowly focused vocational training, but a broad-based liberal arts and sciences education. We are not doing our youth a favor by preparing them for their first job, as many parents want us to do. We should be preparing them for a lifetime of many different jobs. Indeed, we should really be preparing them for their *last* job.

Even though they are studying a classical curriculum featuring books that were written hundreds if not thousands of years ago, St. John's students, whether or not they are willing to admit it, are being given the tools and skills they will use for the rest of their lives. They are learning how to reason logically as well as morally, how to think critically and analytically, how to communicate clearly and effectively, and how to live as good citizens not only in our democracy, but also in an increasingly diverse global society. Perhaps these students are not taking courses that will prepare them for specific careers or vocations. Many will go on for postgraduate training, which is increasingly necessary in the complex and highly technical world we live in. But my bet is that most employers are quite happy with the St. John's graduates they hire, simply because Johnnies tend to be extremely intelligent self-starters who conquer new challenges very quickly.

This said, preparing students for jobs and careers has not always been a strong suit of most liberal arts colleges. Before the 1980s, for example, career counseling was only done as an afterthought. Little effort was made to help students find employment if they decided not to go on to graduate or professional school.

The problem, I think, was that many faculty in those days believed that you attended college for the pure joy of learning. They often pointed to the ancient universities, places like Oxford and Cambridge, as models for what the modern academy should be, namely, a place that stressed the ideal and underplayed the practical. In their opinion, career planning offices compromised the purity of what went on in their classrooms and labs. In all the four years I attended college, I can't remember hearing a peep about what I might do after graduation beyond a professor or two who talked to me about graduate school possibilities in my senior year. And if there was a career planning office on campus, I was unaware of it.

But this kind of thinking was terribly misguided. For one thing, the ancient universities were never detached from practical concerns like the gainful employment of their graduates. The end result of the trivium and quadrivium (the old name at Oxford and Cambridge for the liberal arts) was a career in law, medicine, or divinity. Indeed, the university's primary purpose was to prepare people for productive careers *in addition* to providing a broad education.

With tuitions skyrocketing throughout the 1980s and '90s, things began to change. Parents became increasingly concerned about the employment prospects of their children graduating from college, in large part, I suppose, because they didn't want them hanging around the house forever. As a result, liberal arts colleges like St. John's created internships and beefed up their career services operations. Today, career planning is an important activity on most college campuses.

Based on my observation, St. John's students seem to think about careers at three levels of consciousness (some might say unconsciousness). First, there are seniors who don't have a clue what they want to do after graduation, like my rowing companion Jackie. Jackie is an example of a parent's worst nightmare. What mother or father wants to continue supporting their children after doling out more than $100,000 for their education? Then there are students who have a vague notion of what they might want to do after graduation and just need help developing their thoughts. These students represent the largest group at St. John's by far. Finally, there are students like Sara, who had a general notion of what they wanted to do even before they arrived on campus.

The mission of the career services office at St. John's is to reach out to all three categories of students, getting them to begin thinking about life after college at the appropriate time and then, by the senior year, helping them to apply to graduate or professional school or provide contacts, often through internships, that might result in a job. In many ways, students from St. John's face a special challenge because, unlike most colleges and universities in America, St. John's does not have majors or departments, and it's usually through a major that students begin to see what they might do with their lives. The career services office and the college's internship program, then, take on a special significance.

They have done a good job. The "products" of a liberal arts education are the college's alumni, and St. John's alumni have done extraordinarily well not just in education, where many of them end up, but also on Wall Street, in publishing, in law, in the health care professions, and even as research scientists (lending further credence to the belief that St. John's can succeed in teaching science from the Great Books). Some alumni—and Lisa again comes to mind—might gripe about the lack of "practical" preparation they received in their course of study at St. John's. But my bet is that most graduates of St. John's would attribute their success in life to the rigor of a curriculum that made them think for themselves and, more recently, to the career guidance they received from faculty and administration alike.

. . .

It's pouring rain again this morning, so Mr. Pickens announces that we will do exercises in the gym. Groans are heard from the veterans. I overhear one senior telling a group of anxious novices, "You think rowing on the Severn is hard? Just wait till Pickens gets you into the gym." Being a novice myself, I'm not sure what this means.

We enter Mr. Pickens's temple and solemnly take off our sneakers. Coach then asks us to sit before a large blackboard. On it is written a student's rather crude translation from Greek of a line spoken by the chorus in Sophocles' *Antigone.* The verse describes how many of us are feeling on this stormy morning. It also serves as a reminder that there really is a symbiotic relationship at St. John's between what we are doing in sports and what we are reading in seminar.

> Many are the wonders, none is more wonderful than
> what is man
> It is he who crosses the sea
> With the south winds storming and the waves swelling
> Breaking around him in roaring surf

Tom, the senior captain who gave me rowing instructions the other day, jokingly suggests that Mr. Pickens translate this verse back into Greek for us. My bet is that he could do it. But Coach passes on the challenge, and instead breaks us up into teams of seven.

He tells us that each team will spend five minutes at six different exercise stations around the perimeter of the gym: rowing at the erg machines, doing sit-ups, lifting weights, doing jump-ups and push-ups, and finally running around the wooden track that circles above this ancient facility. My team is made up mostly of upperclassmen, including Thom, a big, athletic-looking junior from Portland, Oregon. Everyone seems to know him, and he has a great sense of humor.

Considering my age, I am doing remarkably well. The weight station requires us to bend over a bench holding two twenty-five-pound hand weights while our feet are being held down. We then move from the bent position with our head facing the ground to a position level with the bench. This exercise is somewhat difficult for me because of my inflexible back. The four laps around the gym, on the other hand, are pretty easy, even with part of my lung missing. I'm a long-distance runner.

By the fourth rotation we are all beginning to understand what the grizzled veterans meant when they said that rowing was much easier. Thom, who is clearly out of shape, is turning green in the middle of some jump-ups. "I think I'm going to be sick," he says. He barely makes it to the apron of the gym before vomiting on the floor of Mr. Pickens's temple. I'm glad I'm not Thom!

By the sixth rotation the team has pretty much had it. I'm one of the few still able to complete each of the tasks, but I am exhausted as well. Fortunately, Coach calls an end to the ordeal and asks us to gather back at the blackboard. Thom has regrouped and sits next to me. His color has returned, but he looks very embarrassed.

Coach tells us what's in store. "From now until Occoquan in November," he says, scanning the group with his hawklike eyes, "Tuesdays will involve slow rowing on the river to improve form. On Wednesday we will do fast sprints. Thursdays, more slow rowing. Fridays, tie racing. And then on Saturday we will row around the island."

"What island?" I think to myself. The only island I am aware of is Kent Island, which would require rowing six nautical miles just to get to it. My insecurities return.

. . .

As Mrs. Kronsberg is arranging her several translations of Plato's *Gorgias* in front of her, someone wonders out loud whether, in light of the subject matter before us—the nature of rhetoric—we should instead be sitting in front of the television watching this evening's presidential debates. The national elections are approaching, and tonight is the first big debate between President Bush and Senator Kerry.

Restrained snickers are heard around the table. "I think we are probably better off here in seminar," Mrs. Kronsberg responds. "At least there are no restrictions on who says what and when." She is referring, of course, to the fact that the national debates aren't really debates at all, but (as one pundit put it) more like joint press conferences. "Unlike President Bush and Mr. Kerry," Mrs. Kronsberg continues, "we can at least respond directly to each other. Anyway, Plato is just as interesting."

Mrs. Kronsberg is saying this partially in jest, but Mr. Holland takes the question far more seriously. "I think the debates *are* important," he says with a poker face, "and I understand that after seminar you can see the replay at 11 P.M. on C-SPAN."

Not a great option, I think to myself, for those of us who have to get up early in the morning to row. In any case, I am taping the debate on our VCR at home so that I can watch it after crew practice tomorrow.

We open our various translations of Plato's *Gorgias,* and seminar begins.

Gorgias is an ambassador from Leontini, Sicily, on a political mission to seek military aid from Athens against Syracuse, the Leontinians' archenemy. He is also a well-known orator—a professor of rhetoric, if you will—who is mentioned in the *Meno* as a self-proclaimed expert on the subject of virtue.

The fictional dialogue begins with a debate between Socrates and Gorgias about the power of oratory and what responsibilities the orator has to his audience. Under close questioning from Socrates, Gorgias has to admit that it is not good for an orator to use his persuasive skills in a court of law or at a political meeting when he is ignorant of the subject matter or when his purpose is to deceive. Socrates argues that in addition to being persuasive, the orator must have knowledge of what he is talking about and also know the difference between right and wrong, good and bad.

Polus, a young orator with a big ego, now enters the debate. Polus suggests, among other things, that orators, like tyrants, have great power and therefore can use rhetoric in whatever way they see fit, even if it results in a gross injustice such as arbitrarily putting a person to death or confiscating his property. Socrates counters by suggesting that it is better to suffer an injustice than to be the author of one, intimating later on that there is a special place in hell reserved for those who commit an injustice and get away with it. The young colt (for that's what Polus's name really means) is vanquished. One can begin to see why Socrates makes people angry with him!

Socrates finally takes on an orator friend of both Gorgias and Polus, Callicles, who thinks that philosophy is child's play and spends a good part of his exchange with Socrates making fun of him. In a sometimes contentious debate, Socrates and Callicles argue over philosophies of life and, by extension, the orator's craft. At one point in the debate, Socrates suggests that it is better for an orator to live a virtuous life and to make speeches about what is best for the citizens of Athens than to live a self-serving life making speeches aimed only at gratifying the citizens and telling them what they want to hear. Socrates asks Callicles:

> Do you think that orators always speak with regard to what's best? Do they always set their sights on making the citizens as good as possible through their speeches? Or are they also bent upon the gratification of the citizens and do they slight the common good for the sake of their own private good, and so keep company with the people trying solely to gratify them, without any thought at all for whether this will make them be better or worse?
>
> (*Plato* Gorgias 502e)

Conversation around the seminar table focuses on Socrates' purpose in engaging these men in debate. Jessie suggests that Socrates' purpose is to use reason to break down the orator's rhetorical shield, behind which there is not much substance. Kristopher agrees, adding, "When orators speak on subjects about which they have little knowledge, they are actually doing an injustice." Nathaniel makes the observation that both Socrates and Callicles are really politicians. "Callicles seems concerned only with gaining power and keeping it, while Socrates cares little about power and only wants to tell the truth."

This conversation creates an image in my mind of politicians across America this election year, most of whom are astute public speakers, appearing on radio and television and in the newspapers. I ask myself whether these people are running for office because they think they can improve America, or because they have big egos and are hungry for power or self-aggrandizement. Will they use their oratorical skills, which are considerable, to tell the truth? Or will they use them to tell people what they want to hear in order to get elected? And what are their priorities? Are they more concerned with providing Americans with *things* or with making Americans better?

I leave the classroom with Garret, the student who avoided conversation with me during orientation at the meeting with the club archons and team captains. Since that time he has become much more friendly, though I can hardly claim him as a buddy. As he often does, Garret is wearing a European football jersey, this one with "Bayern Munich" on the front in gigantic letters.

"How is it going?" I ask Garret, just to make a connection.

"Not bad," he says.

Not wanting our conversation to die with this pleasantry, I ask him, "So, do you like the stuff we're reading?"

"You know, Mr. Martin, I wasn't sure at first how important or relevant all this is," Garret responds as we exit Mellon Hall. "But last weekend some friends and I visited the Library of

Congress, where we saw Thomas Jefferson's library. It contains all the books we are reading in seminar. And there was Plato's *Gorgias,* front and center. I figure that if Thomas Jefferson thought these books were important to read, then they *must* be important."

After crew practice the next day, I replay the Bush-Kerry debate. I decide that Mrs. Kronsberg was probably right.

· · ·

It's Friday night and the beginning of homecoming at St. John's. As I stroll over to Key Auditorium for the weekly Friday evening lecture, I notice that a number of tents have been set up on the playing fields, each one for a class reunion. I imagine that homecoming must be taking place on my own campus as well, but I have been away from Randolph-Macon for three months now, and reunions and other alumni activities in which I normally take part seem so distant. It's nice just being a student and not having to worry about all the grand speeches I must make on these occasions.

The auditorium is packed with both students and alumni from every year. I see some of the old-timers congregating around the first row, no doubt so that they can better hear the speaker. Not far from them are a cabal of younger alumni, closer to my age, engaged in animated conversation. Several rows away from them I spot Mike, the assistant coach, and his wife, Mary. I decide to sit with them.

Foremost on my mind as I shuffle past some of my teammates who are sitting in the same row is whether I have been relegated to sculling by myself on College Creek forever. Mike is painfully aware that I am not happy about this, and so right after I sit down he comforts me with the welcome news that starting in a week or so I will row in either a coxed four or an eight while those who have been rowing in the larger boats will do individual sculling. "Don't worry, Roger," he says. "You weren't singled out by Leo. We had a record turnout this year, and there just aren't enough boats or coaches to go around. The entire team will, at some point, rotate through sculling camp."

Needless to say, I am greatly relieved. I ask Mike, "Then why doesn't St. John's buy a couple more shells and hire an additional coach?"

"Because," he responds, "doing so would run counter to the college's philosophy of athletics, which is that they should remain amateur and secondary to the academic program." I can tell Mike is not speaking with a great deal of conviction. I suspect there might be another reason for not being able to accommodate the entire team, like a tight budget. I can't believe that rowing could ever upstage the Great Books at a college like this.

The loud chatter in the auditorium begins to subside as the president and an extremely distinguished-looking gentleman approach the podium. Mr. Nelson introduces this man as Peter Weiss, class of 1946, a prominent corporate lawyer who also does pro bono legal work in the area of human rights. The title of his address is "Human Rights from Antigone to Rosa Parks." Having just read a crude translation of Antigone in the gym, I especially look forward to this lecture.

What I like about Mr. Weiss's presentation is that not only is it blessedly brief (some Friday evening lectures seem to go on forever), but he brings to life the classics by making them relevant to an important period in my own youth, that is, the civil rights movement of the '60s. Right off, he tells the audience that he believes in discussing philosophical arguments in the context of real events, so I know that I'm in for a treat.

Weiss points out that in classical literature, human rights are informed by three forces: the gods, reason, and a sense of what is just. He then traces these themes from *Antigone* through the literature of the Renaissance and the Age of Reason and up to the civil rights struggle of our own day. By the time he finishes, I have an even deeper sense of why the classics are indeed relevant to everyday life. I feel vindicated, as well, in my own attempt to relate the broad themes I am reading in seminar—themes of life and death, justice and revenge—to the world in which I live, something that is not always permitted by the tutors in seminar discussions.

I look at my watch. It's only 9 P.M. Usually these lectures end at 10, or sometimes at 11. I decide to skip the question-and-answer period in the Conversation Room and instead wander over to the Coffee Shop to check out the social scene. As I get up to leave, Mary calls over, "Don't forget about dinner at our house tomorrow evening."

"I look forward to it," I say, not quite sure what I have gotten myself into.

.   .   .

The Coffee Shop isn't as crowded as it usually is following the Friday evening lecture. There are a few students milling around and some alumni checking out the familiar haunt, but otherwise, the place is kind of dead. I buy a Coke and climb into my usual booth.

Suddenly, I get a whiff of some really bad body odor. Like my dog, I have a keen sense of smell, and this odor tells me that

I'm near the kid who snubbed my attempt at polite conversation at the orientation. It's Phil. He is wearing the same old University of Pennsylvania sweatshirt he was wearing when I first met him.

"Phil," I shout out, once I see him. "What's up?" Phil does a double take and walks over to my table.

"Aren't you the college president who is trying to be a student?" Phil asks. I am amazed. My introduction three months ago actually registered with someone.

"That's me. Grab a seat." Phil somewhat reluctantly agrees to join me. He places on the table Thucydides' *Peloponnesian War,* the book we will be reading more than a month from now.

"I'm impressed, Phil. We don't read Thucydides for several weeks."

"Yeah, I know," he responds. "I've already read Plutarch and Herodotus in a college course I audited during my senior year in high school. I'm just trying to get ahead of the game."

"You're kidding," I respond. "You took a college classics course? Tell me more."

Like Shannon recently did, Phil begins to tell me his life's story, which surprises me, considering how reluctant he once was to even tell me his name. I guess he isn't as shy as I thought, or maybe I'm beginning to fit in and students now see me as just another freshman. Then again, Phil is obviously lonely, with nothing better to do than study on a Friday night. His only options are reading Thucydides or talking to me.

Phil tells me that he went to a public school outside Arlington, Virginia. "High school for me," he says, "was not so much about learning but about memorizing for the SOLs." Phil is referring to the controversial "Standard of Learning" exams that all Virginia public school students must now pass in order to graduate. "I mean, I've always been curious," Phil continues. "I've always had lots of questions. And so by junior year, I began to wonder why I was being required to memorize all of these stupid things. I wasn't really learning anything. And I was bored. Also, I have a passion for conversation, and there wasn't much meaningful conversation going on in the classroom. No one argued or debated issues. We just prepared for the tests. So in my senior year my parents let me audit a classics course at a nearby university."

"So this experience influenced your college decision?" I ask.

"Yes, I suppose it did," Phil continues. "I needed a place that would quench this thirst I had to learn, or at least help me quench it myself. I also needed a place to clear my head and figure things out. I thought maybe studying the classics would do the trick."

"Is that why you chose St. John's?" I ask.

"No. Not by a long shot," Phil continues. "When it came time to consider college, there was only one option for me. Penn. Penn is where my father went to school. Ever since I can remember, he and I went to football games and other athletic contests. My father bleeds red and blue. My room at home was decorated with University of Pennsylvania paraphernalia. Dad loved the place. I hated it." As Phil says this, he seems oblivious to the fact that even now he is wearing a Penn sweatshirt. "And so when it came time, I did what my father told me to do and I applied to Penn as an early admission candidate. Dad was convinced I would be a no-brainer for their admissions office. But he was dead wrong. Even with 1400 SATs and good high school grades, I was rejected. Didn't even get on the wait list."

"Your Dad must have been disappointed, Phil," I say, not

quite sure I want to pursue this issue any longer. "Why did they turn you down?"

"No extracurricular activities," he responds. "Even though I attended a million Penn football games, I wasn't really an athlete myself. I am physically uncoordinated. And I hadn't joined any clubs either. And frankly, I didn't really feel that I was Ivy League material. I didn't look like the preppy Ivy League students I saw whenever I was on campus. My *father* wanted me to go to Penn. I couldn't have cared less." Phil is looking rather distant at this point. "I felt like I was a failure in my father's eyes. And I lost all interest in college. The rest of my senior year in high school was a catastrophe."

"So who cares? You came to St. John's," I say, really wanting to get off the subject of the University of Pennsylvania disappointment, which clearly has affected Phil.

"That's right," he says, with a twinkle returning to his eyes. "At the eleventh hour—well, after college application deadlines had passed—a friend mentioned St. John's and its Great Books program. Knowing little about the place, but loving the classics course I was auditing, I put in my application and was almost immediately accepted. I guess I became a St. John's student by default."

I notice Phil is looking at his watch at this point. "Gee, Mr. Martin. I've got to run. It's almost 10 P.M. and I promised to call a friend."

"Let's talk again," I reply. "I really want to hear more about how you are doing at St. John's." We agree to continue our conversation on another occasion.

I have met many students like Phil: young men and women whose parents push them to attend a brand-name college, even though they might not have the grades or even the interest in attending one of these extremely competitive institutions. Indeed, Phil's dilemma is eerily familiar to my own when I was a young man. My father desperately wanted me to go to Yale, his alma mater. To help me achieve this goal, I was hustled up to New Haven on any pretext—to watch a football game or to attend an alumni reunion—so that by my sophomore year in high school I had only one college in mind: Yale. Unfortunately, it became very apparent by my junior year, if not before, that I had neither the grades nor the extracurricular activities necessary to get into Yale, and I ended up attending Denison.

Unfortunately, as I have just learned from Phil, the pressure to attend an elite college has not abated. If anything, getting into a college rated in the top ten by *U.S. News and World Report* has become even more important in the eyes of most American parents, and the results can sometimes be unfortunate, especially for students who are not up to the academic competition that defines these institutions. Far better for these students to attend a smaller college where they can develop their potential with less pressure and be successful. Even though St. John's isn't easy, its small size and favorable student-faculty ratio provide a much more nurturing environment than usually exists at larger, more impersonal research universities.

Phil is indeed fortunate to have landed at St. John's.

.   .   .

It is time for the first Saturday practice. I *really* don't want to get up at 5 A.M., even though I now know from my conversation with Mike that I will not be in "skulking camp" forever. But I force myself to get up, and when I arrive at the boathouse I discover that the weekend has taken its toll. Christopher isn't present again. This is the second practice he has missed, and I wonder whether he has dropped out for good. Laszlo and some of his friends aren't present either. Laszlo sometimes arrives late, but otherwise he has been a regular attendee.

This morning most of crew, at least those of us not relegated to skulking camp, are scheduled to do a twelve-mile haul up the Severn and then row around the mysterious island Mr. Pickens mentioned during calisthenics last week (I later discover it is St. Helena Island, just off Little Round Bay). Rumors are flying that this row is a real killer, and so I figure that I will probably be better off sculling on College Creek. But because of the number of absences, and to my utter surprise, I am chosen to row in a mixed eight. Mike was partially right. I was the victim of a planned rotation. But even he couldn't have known that I would be rowing in a regular boat so soon.

Mr. Pickens makes a pointed remark as he assigns me to the boat. "No more sulking at sculling, Roger," he says with a smile. He is right. I did not behave well when I was put in the sculling rotation. "Humiliation," I think to myself.

Coach appoints Maia as our cox. Maia is a sophomore whose generous smile displays almost perfect teeth. I have noticed her around the boathouse, sometimes rowing and sometimes coxing in one of the upper-class eights. As she orders us to take our shell off the rack, she exudes confidence, perhaps because she rowed varsity crew in high school and knows what she is doing. Maia is all business.

I'm assigned the number-four position, which means that

during this marathon row, when my half of the boat is rowing to spell the other half, I will act as stroke, or lead rower for those behind me. I wonder whether I am up to this leadership role.

As we pass under the King George Street Bridge and the railway trestle on our way out to the river, I note great activity at the Naval Academy boathouse on the other side of College Creek. On weekday mornings this boathouse is usually abandoned since Navy practices in the afternoons, but this morning it's a beehive of activity. Will we finally see the Navy crew, one of the finest teams in America? I also note that the weather continues to be inclement. It's too early in the morning to see any clouds, but a heavy fog has settled over College Creek, suggesting that worse things might be developing out on the river.

Maia is a no-nonsense cox. Henry, a freshman sitting in the number-seven position who has let it be known that he has done crew before, starts criticizing the rowing of those behind him, including me.

"Don't let your blades drag on the water," he shouts. "For goodness sake, can't you row harder?" he now blusters.

"Shut up, Henry," Maia barks out. "You're neither cox nor stroke. Just mind your business and row."

No more comments from Henry.

As we row past the Naval Academy Bridge, I feel both the water's turbulence and a sprinkle of rain on my back. Then it starts raining harder. Finally, it's raining cats and dogs, making it hard for me to see the Route 50 Bridge. Our shell is beginning to fill up with water.

Mr. Pickens is almost parallel to us in his skiff, but he isn't watching us row. Instead, he is looking into the distance. I briefly turn my head to see what he is looking at. It's a streak of lightning. We are rowing into a major squall!

Coach instructs us to do a quick river turn and we start to head back to the Naval Academy seawall. There are complaints from some of the rowers, including Henry, who want to brave the elements and row into the bad weather, but Mr. Pickens is right: if there is going to be an electrical storm, this is the last place on earth we want to be.

On our way back, Mr. Pickens, always the coach, comments on our form. I draw only a few comments. "Roger, you'll be a whole lot more comfortable if you move your outboard arm between your knees. Now, move s-l-o-w-l-y up the slide and then snap those legs down. That's it. Much better."

As we pass back under the Naval Academy Bridge on our way home, an armada of yellow Navy shells, perhaps as many as seven or eight of them, suddenly appears from out of the squall to our rear, approaching at a very fast pace. Apparently they were also planning to row around St. Helena, and, like us, they decided to return to port. As they speed past, I hear boisterous laughter coming from the Navy shell on our starboard side.

The midshipmen, all men, are getting a kick out of seeing this rather motley collection of Johnnies. And who can blame them? There they are, in their spic-and-span white T-shirts with "Navy" emblazoned on the chest and their dark blue shorts with yellow piping, all looking extremely fit. Here we are, some of us in multicolored T-shirts, others with long hair dripping with rain, some obviously overweight, others rather skinny, some wearing earrings, others sporting tattoos, and one very tired-looking sixty-one-year-old guy with a red beard rowing in the number-four position. At this spot on the Severn

River two navies meet, one grand and eminent, the other rather discordant and ragtag. Admiral Pickens is our fleet commander, driving a battered outboard skiff. The Naval Academy has several admirals, each in a modern launch that looks something like a mini PT boat.

This scene causes me to ponder Plutarch's *Lives of Noble Grecians and Romans,* the book we are currently reading in seminar, and in particular the lives of Lycurgus and Solon, two Greek politicians who embody radically different political philosophies. Lycurgus is regent to the Spartan king and the architect of Sparta's laws, which are austere and unyielding. In Sparta's military society, the individual exists for the state, everyone is alike, and there is no choice. Solon is the lawmaker for Athens. Here society is diverse. Individualism is in, uniformity out. Choice is the currency of the realm.

Sitting in my shell and watching our two very different crews passing each other on the Severn River, it occurs to me that perhaps these two philosophies of society exist side by side right here in Annapolis, Maryland. St. John's, a college devoted to diversity and pluralism and stressing individualism and nonconformity, is Annapolis's Athens. The Naval Academy, with its focus on the military and loyalty to the corps and its stress on uniformity and order, is Annapolis's Sparta. Navy is different from St. John's!

We get back to the boathouse by 7:30. I rowed in much better form than before, so I feel good about myself. After the boat is stored in the boathouse, I ask Maia how far we made it.

"About one third of the way," she says.

"Do you mean one third of the total trip?" I ask.

"No," she says, "one third of the way up the river. The total trip takes about two and a half hours of solid rowing."

Thank God for sending the rain.

As I walk back to the parking lot, I chat with Henry, the freshman who was chewed out by Maia. Henry is a tall, gawky kid with short-cropped hair. Though he claims to be an experienced rower, rumor has it that he just practiced all summer on the erg machines and only *thinks* he is experienced. Even though he is sometimes boisterous and overbearing, he amuses me, in part because he has an air of confidence that I lacked when I was a freshman forty-three years ago.

I notice that Henry is wearing a Yale crew T-shirt, and I ask him where he got it.

"My brother rowed varsity at Yale," he tells me with some pride.

"I bet he is envious of you," I say.

"Why do you think *that?*" Henry asks, puzzled by my question.

"Because now you are rowing and he isn't," I reply. "Also, I bet he wished he could have gone to St. John's."

"Yeah, right," Henry says in disbelief.

Henry is a character.

.   .   .

When Mary asked me whether Susan and I would come over for dinner, I wasn't sure how to respond. I have tried to remain faithful to my mission to become a college student again and not fraternize with the establishment. I feel okay spending time with Mary. She rows and coxes with the rest of us, so I consider her a teammate. Indeed, she has been especially charitable and understanding when I have screwed up, either because she feels sorry for me or, more likely, because she better identifies with a fellow boomer. On the other hand, I'm a bit nervous about socializing with Mike. After all, he is one of my coaches, and team members don't fraternize with their coaches. So Susan and I pretend that we are having dinner with a fellow student and her husband and try to forget about who Mike really is.

Susan and I walk up to Mike and Mary's house just off West Street, not far from our own home. We settle in for a glass of white wine and begin to chat about where we all came from when the telephone rings. Mike answers it. "Right, Leo, the Martins are here. Come on over."

My heart sinks. My coach is coming to dinner! The man who questioned whether I should go out for crew in the first place. The man who relegated me to skulking camp. The man who is always yelling at me when I am not snapping my legs down. How am I going to pull this off? Am I a student tonight or a college president? What do I call him? "Mr. Pickens," as I normally do? Or "Leo"? And what do we talk about? How godawful I am at rowing, or about the weather?

Soon Mr. Pickens arrives with his wife, Valerie, a no-nonsense businesswoman who is herself a graduate of St. John's. Leo and Valerie greet Susan and me warmly. We all chat about the renovations Mike and Mary are doing on their house, and about the political debates taking place.

The rules of engagement have suddenly changed. Both Mike and Leo (who attended St. John's at the same time, I learn) seem to be deferring to me as though I were an elder statesman in their midst, which I guess I am. Not a comment is made about rowing, except when Leo and Mike tell some really funny stories about when they were students at St. John's and when they rowed together after they graduated. Later in the evening,

Mr. Pickens dazzles us with some comments about the Greek classics. We are drinking good wine and eating fine food, and the conversation just flows. It's like we are with old college friends, just shooting the breeze. The party is over in no time, and we all say goodnight.

I'm glad I accepted Mary's invitation.

.   .   .

The wind is howling this morning, so I'm not altogether surprised that Mr. Pickens once again restricts us to College Creek. I can only imagine how choppy the Severn River must still be. Since we have some time to kill, Coach describes some drills we will be doing this morning, what he calls "Lady Margarets." Tom, the team captain, is placed on an erg machine to demonstrate.

"Now watch Tom," Mr. Pickens instructs us. "Notice how, in the catch position, he snaps his legs down as he pulls the oar up into his chest and sits up straight, and then ever so slowly slides back on his seat on the release." Tom is in perfect form as he demonstrates what Mr. Pickens is describing.

"Why are they called 'Lady Margarets'?" someone interrupts Mr. Pickens.

A pause. "Because when you visit the queen of England," he finally responds, somewhat tongue-in-cheek, "Lady Margaret, the queen's lady-in-waiting, will tell you that you must have good posture, sit up straight in the chair, and at the same time relax, just like Tom is doing right now. Then, when you bend over to receive tea from the queen, your hands must be perfectly even and still so the tea doesn't spill on her lovely Persian rug. Got it?" Everyone nods as though they understand, I suppose because everyone in the boathouse except me has had tea with the queen of England—at least once.

Coach assigns us to the boats. My friends Christopher and Laszlo have just returned from playing hooky, so they are assigned to skulking camp as punishment. I draw an all-male novice eight with Maia at cox again. I see some familiar faces in my boat. There is Robert, the transfer from Santa Fe with the silver ring coiled through his lower lip, sitting in the number-seven position. Thom, who vomited on the floor of the temple, is assigned stroke. I'm assigned the number-two position. I don't know the names of the other guys yet; they're just familiar faces from the boathouse.

We row up and down College Creek practicing our Lady Margarets. My boat is full of young men with plenty of testosterone, so to show how macho they are, many of them are pulling as hard as they can but not bothering to listen to Maia or watch Thom. Everyone, including me, is out of sync. Forget about having tea with the Queen.

There is some commotion in the stern of our boat. I can't see what's going on, but it causes Mr. Pickens to motor over in the skiff. We are well up College Creek, several meters past the Rowe Boulevard Bridge.

"What's wrong, Maia?" he calls over his bullhorn.

"Number seven needs to pee," she yells out, obviously not relishing this ticklish situation.

Coach rolls his eyes. "Can you hold it in?" he asks Robert, who is looking quite embarrassed.

"No, I can't," Robert replies with a convulsive grimace.

I can only imagine what Robert is going through. Here he is, in the middle of College Creek, and he has to relieve himself.

But almost directly in front of him is a woman. What's a guy to do?

"Take the boat into the cove over there," Coach instructs Maia. "And be sure to divert your eyes. Promise?"

"Promise," she says.

Unfortunately, as we row into the cove, Robert is not only in full view of Maia, but also in sight of the sloping lawns of Calvary United Methodist Church, perched high on a hill overlooking our location. These two deterrents are enough to make Robert forget he has to urinate. So the spectacle I was hoping to witness never happens.

Later, back in the boathouse I approach Maia. "Would you have looked the other way, Maia? Fess up."

"Of course I would have," she says, looking somewhat embarrassed. Maia is not only a great coxswain, but an honorable one as well.

I leave the boathouse with our stroke, Thom. To make polite conversation, I ask him what he plans to do after graduation.

"Scientific research," he says. "I've always wanted to be a research scientist."

"Do you think you have been prepared well here to go to graduate school?" I delicately ask. "I mean, St. John's doesn't exactly have science majors."

"You've got to be kidding," Thom replies in disbelief. "Sure, most college science majors take very advanced courses, but they really don't understand the basic principles of science. Hardly any of them read the original works of Huygens, Taylor, Euler, Bernoulli, Faraday, or Maxwell. We do. In my opinion, I've been *very* well prepared."

St. John's students don't lack confidence. On the other hand, I wonder if he is right. I remember Lisa's comments about the St. John's curriculum and her concern about not only whether St. John's students are being adequately prepared for the twenty-first century, but also whether faculty without advanced degrees in science can or should tutor the subject. Fortunately, I am about to find out for myself. Tomorrow afternoon I will visit Mr. Holland's freshman science lab.

. . .

At his request, I arrive at Mr. Holland's science lab a few minutes early so that he can review with me what the class has been doing. The lab resembles a typical seminar room, with a large square table surrounded by wood-framed rush chairs, except that off to the right are lab benches with stools and built-in sinks.

Mr. Holland explains that the class has just finished reading selections from the works of Galen, the second-century Greek physician whose theories about the function of blood were authoritative for roughly 1,400 years. The students have learned that Galen was primarily interested in nutrition when he examined the organs involved in blood flow. Galen suggested that the food people ate was ultimately transformed into blood by the liver. This "nutritive" blood then flowed from the liver to the body, helping to regenerate worn body parts. Some of this blood also flowed to the heart, where it mixed with air from the lungs, creating what Galen called "vital" blood. Mr. Holland tells me that the class is now halfway through William Harvey's *An Anatomical Study of the Motion of the Heart and of the Blood in Animals,* first published in 1628. He says that Harvey observed many of the things Galen did and, in fact, relied on Galen to support some of his own observations. But Harvey's reinterpretation of known facts along with some new observations led to our modern knowledge of the human circulatory system.

I immediately appreciate the strategic way science is being taught here. The curriculum doesn't assume that the students automatically understand the theory and biology behind the human circulation system. Instead, these kids are able to get inside the minds of the great thinkers and discover for themselves how scientific breakthroughs happen.

Soon the students enter the room. I don't know any of them. They quietly sit down around the table and open Harvey's *An Anatomical Study* to a diagram of a cow's heart. Lab begins with a student sitting next to me confessing frustration with Harvey's treatise. "I have read it over and over, Mr. Holland, and I still don't get it," he says in exasperation.

Mr. Holland responds, "That's fine, because today we are going to dissect an actual cow's heart, which might bring Harvey's treatise to life for you." As he says this, a sophomore lab assistant enters the room with a tray of cows' hearts, one heart for every two students. The students choose partners and disperse, two to each side of a workbench. With *An Anatomical Study* open in front of them, they proceed to cut the hearts open following Harvey's seventeenth-century diagrams. As they do this, Mr. Holland walks around to the various workbenches, responding to the students' questions and asking questions of his own, much as he does in freshman seminar when we are discussing Plato or Aeschylus. I follow him like a puppy dog.

Once the cows' hearts have been carved up—not a pretty sight—the assistant returns to the lab with an uncut heart and demonstrates with a water hose exactly how the heart valves operate. You can see from their faces that Harvey's theory has suddenly become crystal clear.

I get an opportunity to talk to the assistant as lab begins to wind down. He is absolutely excited about the way St. John's teaches science. Like Thom did yesterday morning, he exudes confidence that he understands the anatomy and biology of the heart better than students taking a conventional science course in which the professor lectures and the students memorize concepts in order to pass exams.

After the students leave I have the opportunity to discuss with Mr. Holland how science is taught at St. John's. He is not a scientist, of course. Far from it. He holds a PhD from Emory University in comparative literature. And yet here he is in the lab asking helpful questions and opening up paths of enquiry.

Most faculty without science degrees—certainly those at the institutions with which I have been associated—would say that they are not qualified to teach a subject like this, but Mr. Holland has no problem with it. "In our lab," he says, "we approach Harvey's treatise as an elemental and foundational work. Conversation with the students about Harvey's book comes naturally because we are all eager to learn the elements, principles, and procedures of scientific enquiry, and because we are all partners in that learning activity." As he says this, I recall Eva Brann's words on the same subject, which were almost exactly the same. He then mentions the weekly meetings, also described to me by Miss Brann, at which a knowledgeable colleague goes over the experiment or the lab format and answers any questions relatively new tutors like Mr. Holland might have.

It again occurs to me how different this method of teaching

is. At most colleges, professors lecture in their narrow area of expertise. A humanist, therefore, wouldn't be caught dead teaching biology or physics. But at St. John's the tutors are not necessarily considered the experts in the fields they teach. The text is the expert. The tutors just guide the conversation. Doing this well, of course, takes great humility. It means that a tutor might, from time to time, not completely understand a passage or a concept being discussed in seminar or lab. When this happens, the students and the tutor become partners in learning. It's not just a one-way street.

The hour is late, and I thank Mr. Holland for the privilege of being in his class, if only for a day. I now feel a bit better about the way science is taught at St. John's, although it's still not altogether clear to me how well Thom has been prepared to pursue a career in science. The proof are the alumni, of course, and quite a few St. John's alumni have done well as scientists and physicians. What I *am* pretty sure of is that those St. John's students who choose not to become scientists or physicians will have a much stronger background in science and math than their counterparts at most American colleges and universities, where the science and math requirements, if they exist at all, often consist of one or two random courses. Nationally, we are not doing as well as we should in the area of science and math education, but St. John's Great Books curriculum is at least one positive response to this challenge.

. . .

I am standing at the top of Main Street, Annapolis's main drag, which runs from St. Anne's Episcopal Church down a hill to the harbor and docks about quarter of a mile below. From my vantage point, next to the redbrick Maryland Inn, Main Street is like a long, narrow funnel with upscale stores, bookshops, art galleries, and fancy restaurants lining both sides and a panoramic view of the harbor at the other end. The large white cupola of the State House can be seen just over my left shoulder as I begin my trek down to the harbor, where I plan to meet Susan for some ice cream at Storm Brothers Ice Cream Factory, an Annapolis institution. I pass Chick and Ruth's, a deli that has been on this street forever, then O'Brien's Oyster Bar, one of the many fish restaurants in this Chesapeake Bay town, and then cross the street into a small pedestrian park along "Ego Alley," the nickname given to the harbor because wealthy people park their huge yachts here just to be seen.

The sidewalks are teeming with people, including large numbers of Naval Academy freshmen, known as plebes, who are trolling the streets in their white uniforms. Like the owners of the large yachts docked in the harbor, the male plebes want to be seen as well, especially by available young women who seem to descend on Annapolis whenever Navy has a home football game.

As I start to walk toward Dock Street, I see Sheldon sitting on a concrete bench conversing with what seems to be a group of people looking out over Ego Alley.

I'm thinking that maybe Sheldon has finally made some friends, but as I get closer to where he is sitting, I notice that his "friends" are four life-size bronze statues. The largest statue is a likeness of Alex Haley, the author of the best-selling historical novel *Roots*. Seated at Haley's feet are three small children, also sculpted in bronze. Haley appears to be telling these children the story of the novel's hero, his ancestor Kunta Kinte, who arrived at this dock in 1767 as human cargo aboard the slave ship

Lord Ligonier. The memorial I am now viewing is a pleasant surprise to me. That Sheldon is surrounded by four inanimate bronze statues is not.

Sheldon spots me and beckons me to join him on the bench. He is holding a cell phone in his left hand.

"What's up, Sheldon?" I ask, suspecting nothing out of the ordinary.

"Oh, I've just been talking to my mom," he stutters. "I've decided to leave St. John's at the end of the semester. I'm just not very happy here."

"I'm sorry to hear this," I reply, not completely surprised. Sheldon really looks glum.

"I guess I'm just not interested in Greek philosophy and so much reading. And I really miss my folks. I never wanted to come east in the first place. Mom and Dad wanted me to come."

"So what are your plans?" I ask Sheldon.

"Well, you know we live on a farm, and Dad always wanted me to become a large animal vet. I was just talking to my high school guidance counselor back home, and he is suggesting that I transfer to U.C. Davis. It's only a few miles from home, and they have an excellent vet school I can eventually go to. But I'll start out at the College of Agricultural and Environmental Sciences. At least that's what I think it's called."

"That's quite a big change," I say. "I mean, moving from Greek philosophy to agricultural science."

"I know," Sheldon responds, "but I sometimes wonder whether I'm just giving up. But Dad has made up my mind for me."

As we sit discussing Sheldon's plans to transfer, my mind races back forty-three years to my own freshman year at Denison. It must have been about this time of the year when I began to wonder if I could make it at college. Denison wasn't the problem. It was really a wonderful place, and the professors were all very caring, even Mr. Cunningham, my nemesis in Western Civilization. But, like Sheldon, I continued to be extremely homesick for my parents, who seemed to be living on the other side of the planet. I wasn't very popular with my classmates following the D-Day fiasco when I lost the relay race for my freshman residence hall. I was also a very slow reader and couldn't keep up with the reading assignments in Denison's very demanding classes. Because of all these things, my grades suffered, and I felt like a loser.

Sheldon is me when I was his age. He is feeling like a loser as well. He knows that he must leave St. John's, but he feels guilty about his decision. At least he thinks he knows what profession he wants to pursue. I didn't have a clue what I wanted to become, or indeed whether I had it in me to become anything.

I am late for my rendezvous with Susan, and so after talking with Sheldon for an hour, I excuse myself. I feel terrible. I had so much hoped that Sheldon would do better than I did overcoming this hurdle in his life.

. . .

As I enter the boathouse, I notice a large blackboard with boat assignments. Mr. Pickens and Mike must have been up all night figuring out who will row where.

The boat I will be racing in at the Severn Chase and Occoquan has been set. Unless something drastic happens, from now on I will be rowing in the number-two position in an eight-man novice shell called the *Harriet Higgins Warren*. I am pumped!

With the exception of Maia, a veteran of crew from her high

school days in Virginia, we are all beginners. Thom, my friend from Portland, Oregon, who aspires to be a scientist, again sits at stroke, and Robert, the Santa Fe transfer from Little Rock, Arkansas, is right behind him at number seven. Thom is a junior and Robert a sophomore. The rest of the crew are freshmen: Charles, from Bethesda, Maryland, sits at number six; Jack, from Ellensburg, Washington, is at number five; Charlie, from Gaithersburg, Maryland, is at number four; David, from Somerville, Massachusetts, is right in front of me at number three; and Isaac, from Oak Park, Illinois, is right behind me at the bow position. We are a veritable national team, with rowers from all parts of the United States.

In addition to our boat, assignments have also been made for a women's novice eight, a varsity men's quad, and two coxed fours. The quad and one of the women's fours are made up of experienced rowers. The other women's four is made up of freshmen.

We are waiting for Mr. Pickens's command to take the *Harriet Higgins Warren* off the rack, but he is standing in the middle of the boathouse, clipboard in hand, looking around as if he were lost in Grand Central Terminal. "Where is Chris?" he yells out.

Chris is a junior whom Mr. Pickens has assigned to the women's novice eight as its cox. A short guy from Cleveland, Ohio, with blond hair and an angelic face, Chris is nevertheless a big man on campus because he is involved in *everything*. He is editor of the *Gadfly,* the student newspaper, chairs the Student Committee for Instruction, sings in the St. John's chorus (the big one, not the community group for which I auditioned), and serves as a student representative on the Faculty Advisory

Committee for the Mitchell Art Gallery. He also holds down a part-time job in the Communications Office. No wonder he is missing from crew. He is probably sleeping late because of sheer exhaustion.

"Where is Chris?" Mr. Pickens bellows out one last time. "His boat can't launch until he is here."

Some of the novice women are looking anxious. "We don't know," responds Michelle, stroke for the women's novice eight.

"Then go up to the dorm and get him," Mr. Pickens yells back, obviously frustrated by the number of no-shows. "From now on, if one of your teammates doesn't show up for practice, the whole team goes up to the dorm and pulls the villain out of bed." Michelle and her teammates exit the boathouse for the men's dorm.

After they leave, Mr. Pickens lectures the rest of us on our new oars and how they should be used. We have graduated from using Macon blades to using hatchet blades. Macon blades are tulip-shaped and symmetrical. They are easier to slip in and out of the water than the more sophisticated hatchet blades, which are rectangular and broader. When used properly, however, hatchets provide significantly more forward momentum.

I am half asleep from staying up last night reading the first several chapters of Herodotus's *History,* so while Mr. Pickens is lecturing us, I am daydreaming.

One thing a freshman doesn't want to have happen is to do something stupid that draws his classmates' attention, like the freshman woman who arrived in the wrong seminar room the first day of class. Well, it's my turn this morning.

We have launched the *Harriet Higgins Warren* into the inky darkness of College Creek and are idling about two hundred feet from the dock. As we wait our turn to row under the King George Street Bridge, Isaac, the freshman rowing behind me, taps me on the shoulder and says, "Roger, you are rowing with the wrong blade." Because I did not listen to Mr. Pickens's lecture, like the rest of my crewmates, I indeed picked up a hatchet blade designed for someone rowing on the starboard side of the boat. I row on the port side.

"Maia," I say in a whisper, praying that none of the other boats will hear me, "I need a new oar." Tortured groans are heard from my crewmates.

"What did you say, Roger?" she blasts back over the cox box.

"I have the wrong oar, Maia," I respond, still whispering.

This early in the morning, the water is absolutely flat on College Creek, so even whispers can be heard by anyone within several hundred feet of our boat.

"What's going on over there?" Mr. Pickens asks over the bullhorn he always carries with him. "There shouldn't be any talking in the boats."

Maia yells back to Mr. Pickens, this time using cupped hands. "One of my team has the wrong oar." I wish I could disappear.

Mr. Pickens, barely visible in the early dawn, yells back over the bullhorn, "Whose oar is it?" I cringe.

"Roger's," Maia responds. I'm dying.

Mr. Pickens proceeds to pick the correct oar off the dock and has climbed into his skiff. He doesn't bother to start up the outboard motor. Instead, he is now standing on the prow of the skiff with the oar in both hands and, like a Venetian gondolier, he uses it to paddle the skiff slowly toward our boat, singing in Italian as he does it. "'O sole mio," he warbles. My crewmates and everyone else on College Creek double over in laughter as we trade oars. My face has turned bright red, but fortunately it is concealed by the early morning darkness.

It's an absolutely beautiful morning as we row out to the Severn. The sun is just about to rise above the bay. The stars are still bright enough to be seen in the dark purple of the Chesapeake's eastern sky, and there isn't a cloud to be seen. Bobbing sailboat masts look like black sticks in the distance, and in my mind's eye I can imagine the port of Aulis, and Agamemnon and Menelaus leaving for Troy with the Greek armada to do battle with the Trojans and win back Helen. The scene evokes Mr. Pickens's memorable words uttered over a month ago about there being nothing like "being out on the Severn at dawn on a crisp fall morning, watching the sun rising from the east and the geese flying to the south as eight oars move in perfect unison over glistening water." The geese are nowhere to be seen, but our oars are moving almost in perfect unison as we glide out of College Creek and up the Severn.

Coach orders us to slow down as we approach the Route 50 Bridge. David, who is sitting in front of me and who sometimes cranes his neck to see where we are going, suggests that everyone in the boat turn around so that we can see what is coming at us.

Out of the dark we see about ten Naval Academy eights gliding toward us in pairs in perfect order, each eight in front of the other by half a boat length, the oar blades almost touching. They remind me of the Navy's precision flying team the Blue Angels, and we are all truly impressed. These are the future naval officers who will defend our country if necessary. I'm glad they have the latest equipment, and that they look professional as they row. I don't think the students in my boat would want it any other way.

As we get beyond the Route 50 Bridge I look up and see an incredible traffic jam a hundred feet above us. It's the 7 A.M. rush hour, and I feel lucky to be rowing in my shell, far from the madding crowd, simply enjoying the morning.

We are now gearing up for next weekend's Severn Chase, our race with the Annapolis Rowing Club, and so our little armada of two eights, two fours, and one quad prepares to race full speed down to the Naval Academy seawall, twenty minutes of all-out effort. As usual, we start out in a staggered fashion, with the novice women's four going first, then the novice women's eight, then the varsity women's four, then us, and finally the varsity men's quad. We have a twenty-second lead on the varsity quad.

We are rowing really well, and we know this for two reasons. First of all, Mr. Pickens is not yelling at us as much as he usually does. More importantly, halfway between the Route 50 and Naval Academy bridges we have passed all the other boats in front of us. Only the men's varsity quad stands between us and a glorious victory.

We are now rowing at a pretty hectic pace. Our instructions were to begin rowing at a rate of twenty-two strokes per minute, increase to twenty-four strokes after the Route 50 Bridge, and then finish off the last five hundred meters, or the length of the Naval Academy seawall, at top speed. None of us is sure what "top speed" means, but as we approach the seawall, the varsity men's quad is gaining on us. This is the boat with the big guys, the ones the freshmen look up to and hope one day to be in their place. Maia tells us to pull on our reserves. We all see that with a bit more effort we can win, something we have not yet been able to do. I pull hard. So does everyone else, and we cross the finish line half a boat length ahead of the varsity men. We all feel tremendous exhilaration—and exhaustion. We have finally won a race.

As we gather for calisthenics behind the boathouse, Mr. Pickens announces that we will probably row the Severn Chase in the boats we raced today. Then it dawns on me. *I will be racing in a real regatta!* Me, a sixty-one-year-old college president whose glory days on the playing field took place thirty-six years ago. Once I recover from this epiphany, I settle into the hard reality that for the next couple of weeks I will need to focus all of my energies on racing. Why? Because I'm part of a team, and I can't let my teammates down.

CHAPTER 6

Old Farts

When I think of Herodotus, whose *History* we are now reading in seminar, I think of a very old man with a long beard and a wrinkled face. Perhaps this is because I stand in a long line of historians going back to Herodotus, who was arguably the very first historian. Perhaps it's also because right now, as I study and play with the youngsters that surround me, I realize that I must look to them as Herodotus sometimes looks to me—as an old man with a beard and a wrinkled face. In any case, Herodotus is my muse. As I write this book, I am, in a sense, writing history. But I am also trying to tell a good story. This is what Herodotus does with great success.

Herodotus's *History* was written between 431 and 425 B.C.E. It ostensibly tells of Greece's conflict with Persia, but it is peppered with asides, some of which deal with myth and personal opinion, others with what modern historians might consider factual history.

It is Herodotus's opinion, for example, that during the siege of Troy, Helen was actually in Egypt, a fact that, if true, calls into serious question Homer's story line in the *Iliad*. Herodotus is a bit more tentative when telling the story of Arion of Methymna, a well-known harp player who, during a sea voyage to Italy, was forced by thieving members of his Corinthian crew to jump overboard. Herodotus writes, "As for Arion, a dolphin, *they say* [he is obviously not too sure of the facts here], took him upon his back and carried him to Taenarum, where he went ashore" (Herodotus *History* I: 24, trans. Rawlinson). However, not even Herodotus can buy the story told of Scyllias, a Greek from Scione, who supposedly escaped his Persian captors by jumping from a ship and swimming *underwater* ten miles!

In many ways, Herodotus marks a milestone in the literature we are reading. In Homer and Aeschylus, the gods play a prominent role in human affairs. They intervene with regularity in the lives of Achilles and Odysseus, Clytemnestra and Orestes. Herodotus, on the other hand, isn't always so sure about these celestial interventions and reports what the gods *might* have done. But more often than not, he simply discounts their importance. For instance, Herodotus discusses a geological formation involving the River Peneus in Thessaly. He writes:

> The Thessalians themselves say that Poseidon made the channel through which the Peneus flows. Their suggestion is very natural; for anyone who thinks that Poseidon shakes the earth and that the earthquake's splits in the earth's surface are the god's work—anyone, looking at this, will say that Poseidon did it. It *is* the action of an earthquake, as it seems to me—this split between the mountains.
>
> *(Herodotus* History *VII: 129, trans. Grene)*

It is also generally conceded in seminar that Herodotus has introduced us to a new literary genre, one that is very different from the poetry of Homer and Aeschylus and even the Socratic dialogues we have also been discussing. For the first time we are reading nonfiction.

So far, this is my favorite book, not only because I am a historian, but also because Herodotus writes about the timelessness of history and the universality of human experiences. So as we read and discuss various passages in Herodotus's *History* in seminar, I am making mental connections between the work and the world around me, including what I am reading in the newspapers.

In one of his many sidebars, Herodotus tells the story of Astyages, king of the Medes, who lived in what is now Iran. When his manservant Harpagus fails to kill the baby Cyrus (Astyages' grandson and an unwanted pretender to the Medean throne), Astyages lures Harpagus's innocent young son to his palace. Here Astyages "cut [the boy's] throat and chopped him limb from limb" (ibid. 1:119). Not leaving much to the imagination, Herodotus then tells us that after roasting and stewing the boy's body, King Astyages makes the grieving father eat his son's remains.

The setting and the sentiment of this story remind me of the barbaric atrocities in the Middle East we read about daily, as, for example, when Muslims in Iraq brutally murder or torture one another because of differences in their faith. But the story also reminds me how this region has had such a long history of hostility and conflict, inspired especially by differences in culture and religion, and how arrogant (or ignorant) it is for Westerners to think that they can resolve thousands of years of revenge and hatred after just a few years of war and occupation.

Herodotus not only writes about human atrocities, but he deals with big egos as well, and in this election year we are hearing and seeing lots of people with big egos! Once our discussion of King Astyages has run its course, seminar focuses on Xerxes, the central character in Herodotus's work. Xerxes is leading the Persian army in a bid to conquer the Greek city-states. He needs information about the enemy, but his many sycophants tell him not what he needs to know, but what they think he wants to hear, namely, encouraging news about how easy victory will be. It is only when Xerxes confronts Demaratus, the exiled king of Sparta, that he gets a candid appraisal of Persia's odds against the Greeks. Demaratus has been spurned by his countrymen—they have questioned his legitimacy to the throne—and so he is willing to become a quisling. Knowing how tough his Spartan kin are in battle, Demaratus tells Xerxes that defeating the Greeks will not be a cakewalk. Even though Xerxes doesn't follow Demaratus's advice—he finally decides to go into battle—he respects Demaratus because, unlike many of his advisors, he is honest and doesn't sugarcoat the story.

When the Persians are finally defeated by a united Greek force at Salamis and it looks like curtains, Xerxes consults with his chief general, Mardonius, on what to do next. Because of pride, Mardonius counsels that the war should continue lest the Persians lose face, an epic example of wishful thinking. In the end, Xerxes loses everything.

Herodotus speaks volumes to our modern condition. How many times have our national leaders sought counsel from their trusted advisors, only to be told what they wanted to hear, not what they needed to hear. Herodotus (and perhaps Thucydides as well) should be required reading for anyone who aspires to national office.

.   .   .

I walk over to the assistant dean's office to pick up the weekly edition of the *Gadfly,* the student newspaper. Because I don't have a proper mailbox, a student services coordinator in the assistant dean's office, a very friendly woman by the name of Carmita, has agreed to save a copy for me when it comes out each week. Unfortunately, the office is closed at the moment, so I wander back down the hall, hang a right, and head for the Fishbowl. I spot a newspaper rack with a copy of the *New York Times* and decide to read it while I wait for Carmita. An article on the front page catches my eye. It is almost as depressing as the news from Baghdad. It reads:

> The University of Colorado is still dealing with damage to its image after accusations of rape involving football players and recruits in recent years. Many of those accusations also involved drinking, legally or not, at private parties and bars. Some critics questioned what kind of message it sent to students that the athletic director was also an owner of Liquor Mart, the town's largest liquor store.
>
> (New York Times, *November 9, 2004*)

I must be living on the other side of the moon, I think to myself. This kind of behavior would be unimaginable here at St. John's—or at Randolph-Macon, for that matter. But before I can get further into the story, I feel a light tap on my right shoulder. It's Phil.

"Funny seeing you here, Mr. Martin," he says, looking somewhat embarrassed. "I felt so bad running out on you the other evening. We didn't finish our conversation. Got a minute now?"

I decide I'll get the *Gadfly* later as we sit down at a table near one of the large picture windows framing the courtyard. Phil places a copy of Plato's *Republic* on the table. I sense he came here to study.

"You were telling me how you got here, Phil," I say by way of restarting our previous conversation. "So, are you glad you came?"

"Love it," he says. "Couldn't be happier."

"Tell me more," I say.

"Well, in the first place I like my classmates. They love to read like I do. Most of my friends in high school hated reading. All they wanted to do was play computer games and watch videos. But my roommate and my other friends just love reading this stuff." He places his hand on the *Republic* as he says this. "And secondly, this isn't my father's college, it's *mine*." Phil emphasizes "mine," letting me know in no uncertain terms that while he loves and respects his father, he is now living his own life. I just wish Sheldon had been able to establish the same independence from his mother.

"Any downside to St. John's?" I ask, fishing for a more critical view of the place.

"Well, yes," he replies. "Dad always wanted me to be a doc like himself. Unfortunately, because pre-med doesn't exist here, you have to take some extra courses in the summer or a postgraduate year. But then again, I'm really not interested in medicine."

"That's okay, Phil," I reply. "What you will become in life is your call, not your father's. Plenty of time to figure it out." I tell

him that a major advantage of a liberal arts education is the opportunity it provides to discover what one's real passion is, and that this probably won't happen for Phil until later in his college career.

I'm beginning to sound like a college president again, because this is what I often say to first-year students at Randolph-Macon, many of whom are egged on by their parents to decide immediately what career they will pursue. "Become an accountant like your dad." "Go into medicine, you'll get rich." "We need you in the family business." This is what mothers and fathers often say to their children when they are in high school.

Sadly, this pressure is not necessarily in the students' best interest. Each year I see freshmen at Randolph-Macon declaring a major in accounting or studying pre-med not because they want to become an accountant or a doctor, but because this is what their parents expect them to be. Often these students don't have the skills, aptitude, or deep interest in the subjects necessary to pursue these rather demanding professions, and they end up hating the education they are more or less forced into.

"Actually, I'm rather interested in history," Phil says, "and I'm thinking about either teaching it or working for a publishing house that specializes in historical works. But I guess you're right. I don't have to decide right now." Phil's got his head screwed on straight.

"Have you visited the career services office?" I ask Phil. I am thinking that Phil fits St. John's middle category, namely a student who has a notion of what he might want to do and just needs some guidance.

"What's *that?*" he replies.

"It's a place that helps students like you plan what they might like to do after graduation. You should consider dropping in on them. They are located in Pinkney Hall." As I say this, Phil is writing the location of the office on the back of his hand, the way teenagers often record this kind of information. I feel I have helped out both Phil and the career services staff by making this connection.

"Have you joined a club?" I ask, changing the topic.

"No, but I'm playing soccer," he responds, "which is really rather unbelievable when you think about it."

"What do you mean?" I ask.

"Well, I never played on an athletic team in my life. I just *watched* with my father. But I really listened to what Mr. Pickens said at orientation—you know, the bit about going out for a sport you never did before—and so I decided to try soccer. I love it. I'm not the greatest player in the world, but I practice hard and I'm getting better. You ought to come out some day and see me play."

"I'll certainly do that, Phil." As I say this, I notice Carmita beckoning to me from outside the Fishbowl. She is returning from lunch and has a copy of the *Gadfly* in her right hand, waving it like she is hailing a taxicab.

I sense Phil really needs to study, so using Carmita as an excuse, I say good-bye and make an exit. But as I do this, I realize that while the plan was for me to become a freshman again, I'm having a very difficult time abandoning my role as an advisor and teacher. (Why should you?)

. . .

This morning is our last practice before the Severn Chase tomorrow. We are all business now. No more messing around.

Everything we have learned comes into play. The Lady Margarets and all the tie races ultimately have one purpose, namely, to prepare us to race. Today we will do one more tie race before the real thing. This is our dress rehearsal.

As my crewmates and I now do each morning when we enter the boathouse, we look for Maia, our cox, and gather around her awaiting Mr. Pickens's order to unrack our eight, the *Harriet Higgins Warren*.

I join Maia and Thom, who are standing together near the open garage doors. Soon Isaac and Isaac's roommate, Charlie, enter the boathouse and walk over to us.

Isaac, who sits in the bow right behind me, is a diminutive kid. He is not very talkative, at least not with me, perhaps because he perceives the presence of an old man in his boat as something of an embarrassment. On the other hand, Isaac is about the last person one would expect to go out for crew. Like me, he looks more like a bookworm than an athlete. Charlie, Isaac's roommate, looks more the part. Charlie is one of our stronger rowers.

I see David near one of the workbenches talking to Victoria. Maia signals him to join the group. As David walks over, Jack emerges through the garage doors of the boathouse from the darkness of College Creek. He has been carrying oars down to the dock, his reward for getting to practice early. Soon Charles, who looks very young for an eighteen-year-old and *never* misses practice, enters the boathouse. Only Robert, the transfer from Santa Fe, is missing.

The women novice eight have just taken their shell off the rack. "Okay, Maia," Mr. Pickens barks, "move your team out."

"Where's Robert?" Thom asks in hushed tones so that Coach can't hear him. Without Robert, we can't launch.

"I think he is in the sack with his girlfriend," Isaac responds with an elfish smile.

"What should we do?" David wonders out loud.

Maia, our leader, decides to approach Mr. Pickens for advice. Coach is now on the other side of the boathouse, near the cluttered workbench, talking to Anna. The cox is the captain of the boat, so it's her responsibility to make sure the team is present and ready to launch.

As Maia walks over to Coach, I join her, wanting to give moral support. I can tell she is concerned.

"Mr. P, we're missing number five. Robert isn't here," Maia blurts out, interrupting Coach's conversation with Anna.

"Then go up to the dorm with the team and yank him out of bed, for heaven's sake," Mr. Pickens responds, seeming put off that Maia even has to ask what to do. Mr. Pickens doesn't seem in a very good mood this morning, and I can't blame him. His frequent lectures about showing up for practice seem to have fallen on deaf ears.

Maia seems in a quandary, and I am as well. I've seen what happens when a crewmember goes missing, but I never thought that I would have to be involved in one of these search-and-rescue operations. And should I be? I mean, is it becoming for a college president to be entering a freshman residence hall with a bunch of angry teenage crewmembers to rouse a sleeping sophomore who might or might not have a female guest in his room?

As my crew leaves the boathouse for Campbell Hall, I approach Coach. "Coach, I really think I should hang back."

Mr. Pickens turns and gives me a scornful look. "Are you or are you not a member of the crew, Roger?" he abruptly asks looking me straight in the eyes. This is not the Leo Pickens I remember from Mike and Mary's dinner party the other night!

"Well, yes," I respond. "I am."

"Then you go as well."

"But maybe he is up there with a girlfriend," I respond weakly, hoping that Coach will let me off the hook.

"Go!" Mr. Pickens barks at me loudly before turning his back on me and resuming his conversation with Anna.

I head out of the boathouse and catch up with my crewmates, who are now halfway up the walk back to campus. Maia tells me that, as a woman, she is very uncomfortable entering a men's residence hall. I share her concern, but for a different reason. I am again remembering the episode many years ago when, as a new college president, I was caught by campus police spying on a freshman mixer. As this dark thought flashes through my mind, I follow my teammates into Campbell Hall, walk up to the third floor, proceed down a long narrow hallway, and wait next to Robert's door at the very end.

Thom, gently at first, and then more loudly, knocks on Robert's door. No response. "Robert, wake up," Thom says, trying not to rouse the entire dorm. Still no response. "Come on, Robert. We can't launch our boat without you. *Please* open the door," Thom pleads, this time with more urgency. Complete silence.

"Let's bust the door in!" yells Isaac at the top of his lungs. For a small guy, he has a huge voice.

I begin to worry about what might happen next. In my mind's eye I see campus security officers rushing down the hallway, billy clubs in hand, arresting the lot of us for disturbing the peace and causing us to end up the next morning in Ms. Seeger's office for disciplinary action and possible expulsion. What would I tell my community back in Ashland if this happens to me?

Fortunately, calmer minds prevail. Isaac and some of the others have calmed down, and we soon come to the conclusion that Robert isn't in his room, or, if he is, he isn't saying anything.

I sigh with relief as we march back to the boathouse. Never, in my wildest imagination, did I think that at age sixty-one I would become part of a posse assigned the task of breaking into a freshman residence hall to wake up a delinquent teammate. What will I do next?

We get back to the boathouse and explain to Coach that Robert is nowhere to be found. Laszlo, who is in the process of pulling a single scull off a sling hanging from the boathouse rafters, is co-opted against his will and assigned Robert's seat in our boat.

The water is fairly choppy as we launch our eight and row out of College Creek. By the time we enter the Severn, we have taken on some water, but not enough to concern us. Our little armada of two women's fours, a men's and a women's novice eight, and the men's varsity quad rows up the Severn, past the Route 50 Bridge, to a point just below where we normally begin our tie races. This has not been easy. The choppy water makes it extremely difficult for us to maneuver the oar blades in and out of the water.

All of us do a river turn and then idle in the water, waiting for Coach's command to start our race. He then tells us that this time we will not row all the way down to the seawall at the normal pace, but instead do a full-throttle sprint to a point a few meters short of the Naval Academy Bridge. I think that he is concerned about conditions on the river.

Running through my mind is how we must look now compared to a couple of months ago. To Mr. Pickens, we must have seemed like a bunch of uncoordinated rookies that didn't know what they were doing. This morning we are skilled, coordinated, and extremely confident veterans. I'm sure that Coach is proud of us.

Mr. Pickens calls out the racing orders. My boat is next to last again, and the race is on.

Despite the choppy water, we have gotten our act together and are purring along like a well-tuned machine—well, maybe like a V-8 Plymouth with one of its cylinders (namely mine) pumping at half speed. We pass the women's eight and two fours as we approach the Route 50 Bridge, but as we emerge from under the bridge, the varsity men's quad is gaining on us. Sure, theirs is a smaller boat, but it *is* the varsity team, so my guys and I are whooping it up, keen to beat our upper-class teammates again, thinking that if we do, anything is possible tomorrow when we are *really* racing. We then race to our finishing point at a speed I have never before experienced, but not fast enough to hold off the varsity quad, which beats us by a quarter boat length. Still, we are feeling pretty good, and we are confident that we will row well tomorrow.

The adventure of the day, however, is still ahead of us. As we head back to College Creek, rowing at a slow pace because of worsening weather conditions, the elements overwhelm us. The choppy water has increased threefold, caused by fairly heavy winds that are now roaring up the Severn from Chesapeake Bay, and we are experiencing rather large swells. As these smash against the sides of our boat, we begin to take on more water. Maia is bailing like hell.

Soon the swells are crashing over our gunwales, and Maia is *really* worried. We can tell she is worried because she is cursing, something Maia doesn't normally do.

But the men's varsity quad, rowing a few feet away from us, is in worse shape. Because they don't have a cox to bail, the water they are taking on is slowly causing their boat to settle lower and lower into the water. A large swell breaks over their bow just as they reach Horseshoe Point, and they are doomed. I watch their boat slowly sink into the water and then completely turn over, taking the crew with it. They are now hanging onto the bottom of the boat for dear life, desperately but unsuccessfully trying to right it.

I hear the groan of Mr. Pickens's outboard motor as he speeds toward the scuttled boat. I am praying that everyone is safe.

Fortunately, the rest of us make it to the relative safety of College Creek as a squall drenches the Severn, causing the swells to turn into whitecaps. All of us are weighed down with water, making our boats look like long, low-lying surfboards. It takes us forever to get back to the boathouse.

As our wounded flotilla rows under the footbridge, I can see Mr. Pickens well in the distance, towing the sunken quad to the shore. Sitting on the deck of his skiff are four shivering upperclassmen.

As we finally approach the safety of the boathouse, I see an omen that could have come straight out of one of the books we are reading. Greek heroes in the heat of battle interpreted natural signs as predictors of victory. I now see one of these signs in the sky above us: I finally see the geese that Mr. Pickens promised on the first day of practice. There are nine of them (like the number in our boat), all honking as they fly south toward Virginia, the direction of the Occoquan Reservoir. Like Odysseus, we have survived Poseidon's wrath, and the vision overhead suggests that we will perform well on the river tomorrow (I don't know why I believe this; it's just a feeling). We can now row in all conditions, in smooth water as well as rough. And we can row pretty well.

Later that evening, I experience a pleasant surprise. My daughter Kate arrives at the house with Ricardo, her new husband. Seeing her just before my first big race is a great comfort. I need someone to talk to, and since Kate has raced many times herself, her presence is a godsend.

In the early evening dusk, the three of us walk down to the boathouse so I can show them the *Harriet Higgins Warren.* I then unload all my fears and misgivings about tomorrow's race, just like I did a couple of months ago when I was obsessing over the two crabs I caught. Once again, I feel like a child seeking the comfort of a parent.

I learn that Kate rowed in the number-two position, just like me. I joke, "Well, I guess the coaches put both of us in the weakest slot." She tells me that this is hardly the case, that the bow and the number-two positions are among the most important in an eight because they help balance the shell. Of course, this is simply her opinion, but she makes me feel pretty important. I then express concern about all the things that could go wrong tomorrow. What if I catch a crab again? What if we get fouled? What if I run out of steam? She puts me at ease by telling me stories of her own misadventures, including the story about when, at a big race at Worcester, Massachusetts, her boat was fouled by, of all teams, the Coast Guard Academy. I remember the event well. After the race she was in tears. She needed consolation. I told her that bad things can happen, but when they do, it's not the end of the world. I was her teacher and coach. Today, our roles have reversed. She is consoling me. Kate is telling *me* that bad things can happen, but if they do, it's not the end of the world. In the seminar of life (as in the freshman seminar I have been attending here at St. John's), the roles of the tutor and student can be reversed. This time, Kate has become *my* teacher and coach, and I feel much better.

. . .

It's early Saturday morning, the day of our first big race. It has been difficult to sleep, and I've been awake since 3:30. In my youth, I experienced this sleeplessness caused by adrenalin coursing through my body just before a big rugby match. But now it's not adrenalin that is keeping me awake as much as it is pain—pain in my back, pain in my arms, pain all over. I struggle out of bed at 5 A.M. It's excruciating just to get my jogging shorts and sweatshirt on.

When I get to the boathouse, it's again like Grand Central Terminal, but with a very different crowd of people this time. On one side are the Johnnies. Except for me, they are all in their teens and early twenties, a ragtag group of young men and women dressed in no particular uniform, a matter of great pride at St. John's. On the other side is the Annapolis Rowing Club, mostly young professionals in their late thirties and early forties (though I'm told by my next-door neighbor on Franklin Street, himself a member of the club, that one of their members is ancient at fifty-eight!). They are all dressed in smart blue-and-white outfits, with "Annapolis Rowing Club" proudly displayed on the back of their team jackets.

On the St. John's side, students are chattering about various subjects. To my right, some upperclassmen are talking about the Friday evening lecture on Martin Heidegger, the German philosopher. I am always amazed that wherever Johnnies congregate, they often talk about seminar or the Friday evening lecture. Another group is complaining about having to get up so early on a Saturday. I notice a student sitting on the floor, deep in sleep, with his back ramrod straight up against the leg of a workbench.

The guys in my eight, including Robert, who has returned from his mysterious absence, are all present. Robert wasn't with his girlfriend after all. He was in Washington, visiting his parents. So much for overactive adolescent imaginations—or wishful thinking.

They are all huddled together near the back of the boathouse, so I join them. Unfortunately, Coach has forgotten to tell us how long the race will be. There is a rumor going around that it will start much further up the Severn than we are used to, so everyone is concerned. I ask Eleanor, a junior from South Africa, whether this is true. She assures me that the race will be the course we normally row, that is, from a green buoy just beyond the Route 50 Bridge to the Naval Academy seawall, or about 5,000 meters.

Justin, who will cox the women's varsity four, has been listening in on our conversation. He has an official map of the course and corrects Eleanor. "Sorry to break the news, guys, but, in fact, we are rowing from here." As he says this he points to a buoy considerably beyond the Route 50 Bridge, some 1,000 meters beyond.

A grizzled veteran who has been listening in confirms that

this will indeed be a 6,000-meter race. My team is in disbelief. "Oh my god," someone behind me says. "6,000 meters? We're all going to die!"

Mr. Pickens asks us to join him near the garage doors. "Okay, listen up. Today is race day. I want you to remember everything you have learned to this point. I want you to do your best. Now the strategy is this: Our course is going to be a bit longer than usual, so I don't want you to burn yourselves out at the beginning. Let's start out at twenty-six strokes per minute, take it up to twenty-eight at the Route 50 Bridge, and then to thirty halfway between the Route 50 Bridge and the Naval Academy Bridge. At the beginning of the seawall and the first floodlight, I want you to pile it on for the last five hundred meters of the race. Now get together with your teams and prepare to launch your boats. The varsity quad will go first."

Maia barks out the usual orders to unrack our boat. We then march out of the garage doors onto the dock and launch. Justin pushes on my oar to move the *Harriet Higgins Warren* away from the dock. Realizing that he was the bearer of bad news about the length of our race, he utters the following words of wisdom: "Good luck, guys. And just remember, this is supposed to be fun."

While we are rowing out of College Creek, which this morning is as smooth as glass, I remember the fantasy I often replay in my mind when watching Randolph-Macon play football: I secretly suit up at halftime and, during the closing seconds of the fourth quarter, kick a field goal without anyone except the coach knowing who the kicker is. This morning I realize that in many ways I am living out this fantasy. I am a ringer rowing in a novice boat, and although I won't kick a field goal, I will have a hand in trying to win this race.

why?

We row and row and row, and then we row some more. We are now well past the Route 50 Bridge and in territory that none of us has ever raced from before. We have been rowing at a rate of twenty-two strokes per minute, a fairly fast pace over such a distance. Finally, we reach a buoy that marks the starting point of our race, 6,000 meters from the end of the Naval Academy seawall and its eighth floodlight.

"How are we going to survive 6,000 meters starting out at twenty-six?" David, who sits directly in front of me, wonders out loud as we await the teams that will race to assemble.

Maia tries to put us at ease. "Don't worry, guys. I don't care what Mr. P says, we'll start out at twenty-four. If we begin any faster, we'll never make it." But we are all thinking that twenty-four strokes per minute might do us in anyway.

By my reckoning, we are just above Clements Creek. A point of land obscures our view of the Route 50 Bridge, making it seem a world away. To our backs is a growing flotilla of boats from both St. John's College and the Annapolis Rowing Club, including four eights, numerous fours, one quad, a couple of doubles, and Henry in a single scull. I can't imagine why Henry would want to row all by himself, but there he is, ready to race along with everyone else.

Idling just a few feet off our port is a men's eight from the Annapolis Rowing Club. The crew, men in their mid- to late forties, are all in a celebratory mood. While my guys are absolutely morose, thinking about the distance they will have to row in a few moments, these veterans of the Severn are telling jokes and laughing. They are having one big party. Their stroke is wearing a beanie with a propeller on the top. The person in the bow position, an overweight man wearing a Baltimore

Orioles baseball cap backwards, is smoking a fat cigar. I'm sure this is meant to intimidate us. Their demeanor suggests, "we're just doing this for fun, but we can *still* beat you children."

The Severn Chase is run like a typical regatta or head race. It is a timed event, with the slowest boats starting first and the fastest boats starting last. The winner is determined by the time it takes each boat to reach the eighth floodlight at the end of the Naval Academy seawall.

Henry, in the slowest boat, will be the first to leave, a couple of minutes before everyone else. Next to leave will be a couple of doubles, then the coxed fours, followed by the eights and finally the St. John's varsity quad, probably the fastest boat on the river today. Within each class of boat, the women will begin before the men, with the exception of the Annapolis Rowing Club's women's eight. Made up of women in their late twenties and early thirties who rowed in college, like my daughter Kate, their boat will go just before the St. John's varsity quad, because it is also very fast.

Our turn soon comes. The Annapolis Rowing Club's men's eight departs, and a few seconds later we are told to take off.

We are off to a good start, rowing at a rate of twenty-four strokes per minute as Maia promised. Unfortunately, the cox box is not working, so it's difficult to hear Maia. To deal with this, the guys pass her commands down the line. When I hear David say, "Roger, we're increasing to twenty-six on the count of four," I know what is about to happen, and I can pass on the order to Isaac just behind me.

We are now within sight of the Route 50 Bridge, but it still seems miles away. We get into a rhythm and just row. No looking at the scenery. No looking at the crab boats. No looking at the pretty mansions overlooking both sides of the river. We just row. Row. Row. Row. The monotonous rhythm of the oars clicking in unison in their locks is almost comforting. Click. Click. Click.

As we approach the Route 50 Bridge I can see Henry, who is well off to our stern, capsize. But to my right I also see the Annapolis Rowing Club's women's eight steaming toward us at an unbelievable speed. I have seen these women on the river before. They practice a good hour before us every morning and are probably on the River by 4:30 A.M., if not earlier. These women are in tremendous physical shape, and now they are rowing almost perfectly.

Maia sees them gaining on us as well and calls for a "power ten" to hold them off. A power ten involves maintaining the same stroke rate but increasing the pressure to maximum when trying to overtake a boat or when holding off a boat approaching from the rear, and then going back to the normal race pressure. We all groan. But the extra effort is for naught. The women zoom past us, and we can only marvel.

But now, as we approach the Naval Academy Bridge, Maia can see just ahead of us the Annapolis Rowing Club's men's eight, the same boat that seemed to be taunting us only a few minutes ago. I can clearly see the man with the beanie. The propeller is going so fast that I wonder why he doesn't take off like a helicopter. We are beginning to overtake them, so we're getting pumped. It has become apparent to us that these men are not in the best physical condition, and that with a little extra effort, we can take them.

It's now a race between us and them. Maia tells us to bring up our pace to thirty strokes per minute, something we have never done before. She is breaking her promise to row only at a twenty-four-stroke pace, but who cares? We are about to beat these guys. Any sense of pain or exhaustion is gone. We are just rowing our heads off.

We are now bow to bow. Robert is yelling like a banshee, and so is Isaac. As I see the next to last lamppost on the Naval Academy seawall to my left, I inadvertently blurt out, "Let's go, guys! You can beat these old farts!" failing to mention, of course, that they've got the oldest fart of all in their own boat.

We fly over the finish line, beating the Annapolis Rowing Club's men's eight by a quarter of a boat length.

All of us are utterly spent but totally exhilarated. I'm thinking that this race is misnamed. It's not the Severn Chase, it's the Severn *Marathon*. But I am elated, and gratified that I finished my first real race without embarrassing myself. I have successfully kicked the field goal I have longed fantasized about.

We have finished with a time of twenty-eight minutes, forty seconds, about the middle of the pack overall. Not bad for a novice boat. I can't wait to tell Kate.

As we slowly row back to the boathouse, I reflect on Justin's earlier words of wisdom, "Just remember, this is supposed to be fun." This race was a challenge for everyone. Excitement had been building ever since Mr. Pickens assigned us to the *Harriet Higgins Warren* several weeks ago. The day of the Severn Chase was festive, with a sense of good-natured competition. The race itself was as exciting as any athletic event I have ever watched or participated in. And we actually did have fun.

After washing down and storing our boats, it's postmortem time. Mr. Pickens assembles the entire crew in the front of the boathouse for an analysis of what happened during the competition. I'm standing next to the garage doors with my crew.

"Let's start with the human submarine," Coach says, and we all laugh, knowing that he is referring to Henry, whose scull overturned at the start of the race.

"I really enjoyed it," Henry responds, stone serious.

"Which part did you enjoy most Henry, above or below water?" Mr. Pickens jokes. More laughter.

"How about the women's novice eight?" Mr. Pickens asks, continuing the review process.

"We were absolutely exhausted," one of the women replies. I had noticed that they finished the race well behind everyone else.

"Well, if you rowed a little harder you'd have finished sooner, and you wouldn't have had to suffer as long," is Mr. Pickens's retort.

When he gets to our boat the reply is fairly unanimous. Charles says he would rate our performance an eight out of ten, but then revises his figure upward to a nine. Everyone agrees.

When we are finished with this self-analysis, Mr. Pickens gets serious and lectures us on boat safety. With the choppy weather the previous day fresh in his mind, he wants to make sure that everyone knows what to do if their boat capsizes.

"Remember, the key thing is to do what?" he asks.

Someone jokes, "Call mom and dad on the cell phone?"

"You stay with the boat," Mr. Pickens says, ignoring the wisecrack. "I don't care if you won an Olympic gold medal for the 1500-meter freestyle. I don't want anyone trying to swim to shore. *Stay* with the boat."

One of the seniors who rows in the varsity quad asks, "What if my ChapStick drops out of my pocket? Should I dive for it?"

"Only if you have more than a quarter of the stick left," Coach jokes. Everyone is in a great mood.

"Okay, now listen up," Coach says, changing the subject. "See these two figures?" He is pointing to a "14/14" and a "560" that he has chalked on the blackboard. "Does anyone know what these numbers mean?" Silence in the boathouse. Coach answers his own question. "The first fourteen means that we have fourteen days left until the end of the season. The second fourteen is the number of days I want *each* of you to be at practice." Mr. Pickens is very serious at this point. "Do you get my drift? No one misses practice from now on. No one! Including you, Robert."

"So what does the '560' mean, Mr. P?" Robert asks.

"Well, 560 is 14 days times 40, the number of people still in the program," Coach responds. "I want us to have a perfect 560 by the end of the season."

"Now I have one final thing to say." We all listen intently.

"Head of the Occoquan is in two weeks, so we have a lot of work to do. But I want you to understand this: for the time being, winning at Occoquan is secondary. What I really care about right now is the effort and preparation each of you puts into practice; that every man and every woman on this team does his or her personal best from now on. Then come what may at Occoquan. Do you understand?"

This is not the kind of speech many coaches would give. In our culture, winning is sometimes everything. But this coach cares more about personal development and character than about winning a particular race. He knows that there are weak rowers (myself included, no doubt) who at most colleges would have been cut from the team at this point in the season. But this is not the St. John's philosophy of sport. Everyone rows, and everyone is expected to excel within his or her own limits.

We all leave the boathouse, tired but feeling that we have accomplished something important.

CHAPTER 7

Community

Plato's *Republic,* the book we are about to discuss in seminar, is a work of digressions and detours from its themes of politics and personal morality. In this sense, it very much resembles Herodotus's *History.* The digression I like best comes at the very beginning. It speaks poignantly to the condition of aging boomers and suggests what might have motivated me to go out for crew.

Socrates wants to know if getting old is difficult. The old man Cephalus, one of Socrates' protagonists, replies, "A number of us, who are more or less the same age, often get together [and] when we meet, the majority complain about the lost pleasures they remember from their youth, those of sex, drinking parties, feasts, and other things that go along with them, and they get angry as if they had been deprived of important things and had lived well then but are now hardly living at all" (Plato *Republic* I: 329a).

Three years ago I decided to start running again. My doctor

at Johns Hopkins encouraged it, I suppose because running had always been such an important part of my life, and my cancer had been in remission for a year. Before my cancer I was famous for competing in 5K runs, in which I always finished at the top in my age class. Running not only energized me and made me feel good, but it created an image of myself that I liked: a president who is competitive in all aspects of his life. Running for me was synonymous with being young and vital.

One day I walked over to Randolph-Macon's Brock Recreation Center, which has a tenth-mile indoor track. Before my cancer, I could do a mile in about seven minutes flat. I was convinced that I would be able to pick up where I left off, or maybe even beat my previous time, but it wasn't to be.

I started running the first lap, a bit slower than usual because I was somewhat out of shape, but as I approached the first turn I noticed a not particularly athletic-looking student huffing and puffing as she struggled to overtake me. "Piece of cake," I thought to myself as I picked up my pace. "I'll lap her easily and feel *really* good about myself." My opponent picked up her pace as well. Ever competitive, I poured on the speed. Now I was the one who was huffing and puffing. She passed me easily just as I completed the first lap. And then she lapped me two more times before I finished my mile.

When I returned home, all I could do was rant to Susan about my diminished virility. I had lost the will to compete. My life was winding down. I had one foot in the grave.

"Sweetheart, you lost part of your lung," she replied with a look of incredulity. "What are you complaining about?"

"But I've never been beaten so badly. Don't you understand?"

The reality, of course, is that I was running against a person one-third my age. Like Cephalus and his cronies, I really *wasn't* what I had been in my youth, regardless of the cancer. I lacked endurance. I was no longer very fast. And I was having a big problem admitting these things. So today, as I read this passage from Plato, I wonder whether I went out for crew to somehow prove to myself that, at age sixty-one, I wasn't completely over the hill.

As I said, this is an interesting digression, but the *Republic* isn't only about aging. It's also one of the most important books on political philosophy ever written. Most of the framers of the American Constitution read the *Republic*—Garret said it was in Thomas Jefferson's library—and its importance to the education of our founding fathers more than two hundred years ago is incalculable. The book also happens to be an integral part of the St. John's experience. I remember Tom telling me that St. John's freshmen can't claim to be true members of the community until they have read Plato's *Republic*. "That's when you become a Johnnie," he had said.

Our seminar is now discussing Socrates' attempt to construct an ideal state—a republic—that embraces justice. Socrates points out that cities are made up of different types of people, each responsible for the well-being of the whole. There are farmers who grow the food, craftsmen who make implements, merchants who sell both, and, above all, the city's ruling class and protectors, the "Guardians." Since most of the students sitting around the seminar table this evening aspire to be members of the ruling class, conversation naturally turns to the subject of leadership.

Mrs. Kronsberg asks the opening question, "How are the

Guardians to be educated for their leadership role in Socrates' city?"

"Well, they must be educated in music, poetry, painting, and so forth in order to have pure souls," Katrina responds.

Katrina almost always gives thoughtful responses to the tutors' questions, and she has obviously read the assignment, but she is only partly correct. The Guardians must also be physically agile in order to serve as the city's protectors. It is the correct balance between academic study and physical agility that concerns Socrates as he discusses this issue with Glaucon, another one of his protagonists, a few pages later. I am wondering if others have spotted this rather interesting dialogue:

SOCRATES: Haven't you noticed the effect that lifelong physical training, unaccompanied by any training in music or poetry, has on the mind, or the effect of the opposite, music and poetry without physical training?

GLAUCON: What effects are you talking about?

S: Savagery and toughness in the one case and softness and overcultivation in the other.

G: I get the point. You mean that those who devote themselves exclusively to physical training turn out to be more savage than they should, while those who devote themselves to music and poetry turn out to be softer than is good for them?

S: Moreover, the source of savageness is the spirited part of one's nature. Rightly nurtured, it becomes courageous, but if it's overstrained, it's likely to become hard and harsh.

G: So it seems.

S: And isn't it the philosophic part of one's nature that provides the cultivation? If it is relaxed too far, it becomes softer than it should, but if properly nurtured, it is cultivated and orderly.

G: So it is.

S: Now, we say that our guardians must have both these natures.

(Plato Republic III: 410c–d)

As I recall this passage, I again appreciate Mr. Pickens's comment a couple of months ago at orientation about how athletics was as much a part of Greek culture and society as political discourse and debate, and that athletics must therefore be taken seriously. If, indeed, these St. John's students are to become the leaders of our nation, then not only must they study the liberal arts and sciences, but they must also engage in physical activity. This balance between body and mind is central to the St. John's system.

But Plato also helps me see the dangers inherent in an overemphasis on athletics. This is certainly not a problem here at St. John's, but it is a trend I see at many other American colleges and universities. Socrates' dialogue conjures up images of too many young athletes who don't earn their college degree, or whose aggressiveness, often related to alcohol or drugs, lands them in jail. I am reminded of the *New York Times* article I recently read in the Fishbowl.

Sebastian seems restless. An older student with a shaved head and numerous earrings and tattoos, he has a deep, clear voice. When he speaks, which is not frequently, the students and especially the tutors seem to listen.

"It's okay to talk about the Guardians," Sebastian says, "but let's not forget that Plato's republic is made up of other people as well." Sebastian's point is well taken. Justice in Plato's ideal city happens when each person—every woman, child, craftsman, ruler, and ruled—does not meddle with the work of others but

supports the community by attending to his or her assigned
task. Sebastian points out that the farmers and craftsmen have a
job to do just like the Guardians, and therefore they should not
be taken for granted. "No one is more important than anyone
else," he says. "If the farmers don't farm, the Guardians don't
eat. Everyone has a role to play in Socrates' republic. Everyone
is important."

I get a sense from listening to Sebastian that he does not come
from an aristocratic background. Indeed, he looks more like a
dockworker than a member of the Young Republicans. Sebastian is an egalitarian. But what he says makes eminent sense.
Seminar itself is like a republic, with each member playing a
critical role. The tutors—Mrs. Kronsberg and Mr. Holland—
are perhaps the Guardians, but each class member makes a distinctive contribution. Some, like Christopher, are helpful by
responding to the tutors' first questions at the beginning of seminar, especially after a long silence. Others, like Nathaniel and
Kristopher, keep the conversation going. Still others are perhaps quiet, but at key times provide deep and profound analysis
of a particularly difficult passage. Sebastian himself often plays
this role. So do Katrina and Tim. Then there are the specialists.
Elizabeth will jump in when issues involving women's rights
are under discussion, and Alyssa is always there to uphold traditional family values. Everyone plays a part, and the result is a
very dynamic and fulfilling experience for those participating— a
true intellectual community.

Emily, who looks as if she were about sixteen years old and is
always well prepared and thoughtful, glosses over Sebastian's
comment. Like most students around the table, she remains
focused on leadership. She points out that Socrates' ideal city

cannot come into being until the king—a leader drawn from the Guardians—is a philosopher. Dan, who is a very quiet but thoughtful participant in seminar, asks Emily to describe this "philosopher-king" Socrates has in mind. Emily, summarizing from her translation of the *Republic,* reels off the attributes. "He should be a person," she says, "who loves learning, who is wise, who is without falsehood, for whom wealth is not important, who is not cowardly or slavish, and who is a fast learner." In short, he should be the kind of ideal orator Socrates describes in *Gorgias,* whose unselfish objective is to build a city based on justice and goodness.

Both Emily and Sebastian are right, of course. Philosopher-kings are important, but without a well-educated and responsible citizenry, each doing their part, the philosopher-king cannot be effective.

. . .

St. John's has its own philosopher-king—well, perhaps a philosopher-king in training—and I meet him on the river this morning.

Maia is out sick, so Joe is appointed cox. Joe is a short kid who often wears a beige airman's jumpsuit, as though he were about to pilot an F-16 rather than cox an eight-man shell. Joe is like manna from heaven for me. He was one of the students whose chatter with Laszlo earlier in the season I found so fascinating. I then made the mistake of telling Mr. Pickens about this sophomoric banter, resulting in an apology from Laszlo the next day. At the time, I felt bad about this. Until I spilled the beans, I had an insider's view of the undergraduate subculture at St. John's. Joe and Laszlo talked back and forth as though I were just another student, and I really enjoyed this anonymity. When they left my boat, I missed their jocular and sometimes off-color conversations. But Joe is back now, as loquacious as ever, and once again I'm just another member of the crew.

As we row, Joe announces that he will be telling us some of his better jokes and also giving his opinion of recent movies he has seen. But first he asks us to count down by shouting out our names starting with the stroke. Rather than referring to us by number, which is Maia's method, he wants to personalize his commands. Instead of "Number two, please row," he wants to say, "Roger, please row." This would be okay, except that Joe can't get our names straight. Moreover, there are two Charleses in the boat (though one is known as Charlie), so when he issues orders to "Charles," Charlie and Charles aren't quite sure who's being addressed.

Joe talks as we row, and as a consequence we are totally out of sync. When he says, "Charles, weigh enough," both Charleses stop rowing, which is not good, since both row on the port side of the boat. I never get called on because Joe can't quite remember my name. Meanwhile, he jabbers away.

During at least two movie reviews and one really great joke, we have done several laps up and down College Creek. All the while, I am reflecting on Plato's *Republic*. Joe's oddball combination of athleticism and pseudo-philosophy seems vaguely in keeping with Socrates' ideal ruler, the philosopher-king. However, in a passage comparing the captain of a ship to his ideal ruler, Socrates suggests that in addition to philosophizing, a true philosopher-king must also "pay attention to the seasons of the year, the sky, the stars, the winds and all that pertains to his craft, if he's really to be the ruler of a ship" (Plato *Republic* VI: 488d).

We begin our sprint. We are now rowing at a rate of twenty-six strokes per minute, a very fast speed on this congested creek. Joe is yelling commands and philosophizing at the same time. As we approach the Rowe Boulevard Bridge, I do something I rarely do. I turn around. To my horror, I see our boat making a beeline for one of the pilings. "We're going to hit the bridge!" I yell out in absolute panic.

Joe cuts short his monologue and yells, "Damn it, weigh enough. *Pull in your oars!*" Two port oars, those of the two Charleses, slam into the pilings as we come to a dead halt.

Joe seems embarrassed and apologizes. But being so focused on liability issues—a subject that is always on the mind of college presidents—I can only wonder what would have happened to poor Isaac, just behind me in the bow, had we rammed full force into the bridge. Clearly, to become a true philosopher-king, Joe will need to do a better job of paying attention to his environment, like the ship captain in Plato's *Republic*.

On our way back, Joe, who is strangely silent now, announces that he might be our cox the next several days, or until Maia returns. The crew cheers. Rowing with Joe is like going to the movies.

. . .

I have arrived at seminar fifteen minutes early. As I stare at the empty table, I think about how happy I am to be here at St. John's. My metamorphosis from a college president to freshman student is almost complete, and I am finally enjoying myself. I'm enjoying being a member of crew. I'm enjoying reading the Great Books. I'm enjoying hanging out in the Coffee Shop and meeting students. I've attained nirvana.

While I am deep in these thoughts, my classmates have assembled around the table and Mr. Holland has begun a discussion of Plato's cave. "Who are these shackled prisoners staring at the wall?" he asks.

In Plato's famous allegory of the cave, prisoners are seated in a single row looking at the wall of a mythical cave. Their heads are constrained so they can only look forward. Directly behind them and moving from one side of the cave to the other is a raised roadway over which travel men carrying vessels and figures of animals made of wood and stone. Still further back in the cave, and slightly above the roadway, is a bonfire. When an object passes from one side of the roadway to the other, the light of the fire projects the object's shadow onto the wall of the cave for the prisoners to see. They can only see the shadows of the objects against the cave's wall, not the objects themselves. For these prisoners, then, the shadows are reality.

One of the prisoners is unshackled and set free. He can now turn around and see the objects passing on the roadway behind him. It takes time for him to realize that these objects, not the shadows he has been seeing all his life, are still a partial view of reality; even these objects are not the real thing.

Soon this prisoner is compelled to crawl out of the cave and into the world beyond. When he does this, he confronts blinding sunlight, which, for Plato, is the light of the good. At first the light is so intense he cannot see anything, but his eyes slowly adjust, and soon he is able to see true reality in front of him. The prisoner has been liberated.

He now thinks about his fellow prisoners. He is compelled to crawl back into the cave and lead them to the light. He has become a philosopher-king.

"The shackled prisoners staring at the cave wall are slaves," Zach responds to Mr. Holland's question. "For them, ignorance is happiness."

"Right," Morgan agrees. "But they are compelled to come out of the cave once they are unfettered and can see reality. There is an innate desire in each person to learn what the truth is."

"But once they see the light, aren't they compelled to crawl back into the cave?" Tim asks.

"Absolutely," Alyssa says on cue. "And once they go back into the cave they can show others that the shadows are not real."

"But they can also regress," Christopher warns the seminar, "and just go back to thinking that the shadows are real. It's often easier to live in ignorance."

As I listen to this chatter around the seminar table I gain a fuller sense of the fickle reality of my own life. My mind goes back to the hospital room at Johns Hopkins where I first began receiving Interleukin II treatments for my cancer. That room was also dark as a cave. I was constrained, only able to move my head to the left and to the right. I remember eerie shadows cast on the white walls of my room with depressing regularity. These shadows included images of all the things I would no longer have should this terrible disease end my life. I would no longer be a person of stature and importance, no longer in control of the destiny of my college, no longer looked up to by the community. And what if I survived? These images weren't much more hopeful. The specter of retirement loomed large on the wall of my cave, with everything that retirement suggested to me: boredom, malaise, apathy, physical inactivity, nothingness. It didn't matter whether I lived or died. Scenarios for both were equally depressing.

But as I attend seminar this evening and reflect on the joy I have experienced here at St. John's, Plato inspires me to wonder whether prestige, stature, and power are really distorted mirages or, at best, only a partial view of reality? I think about what Kate told me over the phone after I caught two crabs earlier in the semester and lost the race for my boat. "Stop trying to control everything. You don't always have to be boss. Just let the oar handle rest loosely in your hands and enjoy life." She was right. I don't always have to be driven and competitive. I don't always have to run things. I wonder whether the St. John's faculty—Professors Homer, Plato, and Herodotus—have entered my own dark, gloomy cave? Did they lead me out of this cave so that I could see a different, perhaps more realistic, vision of beauty and truth?

.   .   .

Susan and I decide to attend another Waltz Party. The last one we tried to attend didn't get started until after 11 P.M., so in preparation for this one we take a long midday nap.

Earlier today I noticed a flyer on the bulletin board outside the west door of the Coffee Shop encouraging students to "dress up" for the Waltz Party. Does this mean to wear sequined dresses and tuxedos, like many students wore last time? Or to dress up like a college student might typically do on an occasion like this? So, instead of the Harris Tweed jacket and gray slacks I normally wear to college events, I put on my finest jeans and a blue denim shirt, like those I often see students wear to the Friday night lecture. Susan buys a new pair of cropped pants just for the occasion. We both think we look pretty cool. Of course, we're kidding ourselves.

We stroll over to the quad at about 10:30 P.M. I spot Annie and Julie sitting on a bench under one of the elm trees. Almost always together, they look like twin sisters to me. Both of them are members of my seminar, and both also row. While Susan goes to the ladies' room, I sit next to Annie and start chatting with her.

"Enjoying St. John's?" I ask.

"Tons," she responds. "Never a boring moment."

"So what's your favorite subject?"

Her answer surprises me. "Freshman chorus," she says.

"There's a freshman chorus?" I ask, absolutely aghast. It's almost the end of the semester, and nobody told me about this. I'm trying to remember my conversation during orientation with Ms. Seeger. She didn't mention freshman chorus. Or did she?

"Oh, yes," Annie replies. "It's a requirement. At first I thought it was a silly requirement, but now I realize what a great thing it is to bring the entire class together in one large singing community."

I'm kicking myself that I didn't know about this. A required freshman chorus is just one more dimension of this wonderful college community. I have missed something very important.

Susan returns before I can find out more. As she grabs my arm I say good-bye to Annie and Julie, and we enter the Great Hall. Unlike the last time, the Waltz Party is apparently starting on schedule.

Once inside we notice that the students' dress is very different this time: there are no feather boas or cloche hats. Heavy metal is more the fashion, but there are also eccentrics. In one corner of the hall I see a kid with long blond hair tied in braids who is wearing a Scottish kilt and waltzing with a woman in a long, black silk evening gown. Coming in the door just behind us is a student wearing a New York Mets uniform with a Louisville Slugger perched on his left shoulder. And here we are, dressed like a hip college president and his wife.

"Love your costume," Anna says as she whisks past me, arm in arm with a young man I have never seen before. She and her escort join a small crowd of people on the dance floor.

At the moment, everyone is doing the St. John's version of the swing, but when the music changes, the students start jitter-bugging. This is fun, St. John's style, and everyone is dancing as if the world were coming to an end.

Off in the distance I suddenly see Auggie and Sara beckoning me to join them on the raised platform at the other end of the Great Hall. Susan and I walk over to where they are dancing. Auggie, a recent St. John's graduate and sometimes-cox, has apparently been dating Sara. I now remember Sara's parting words after our meeting in the Fishbowl the other day. She promised she was going to teach me how to do the swing.

"Come on up here, Roger. Time for swing lessons," Sara says with coxlike authority. Auggie moves off to the side.

I rather awkwardly try to follow Sara's instructions.

"Now hold both of my hands and bring them up like this," she says as we raise our arms like we are playing "London Bridge Is Falling Down." "Okay, when I move my left foot back, you move your right foot forward. Now, swing our arms back up again and do a dip. Just watch how I do it." As I try to follow her instructions I am fouling her with my feet, much like

I fouled her with my oars in the training barge three months ago. Auggie and some of my teammates who are standing nearby howl with laughter as I finally give up and step off the platform.

As this laughter fills the air of the Great Hall, I am again transported back to 1961 and my freshman year at Denison. Greek rush was about to begin. Desperate to be accepted by my classmates, and wanting to stop feeling sorry for myself, I had high hopes of being tapped by a fraternity. Maybe by going Greek I would get over my insecurities, overcome my shyness, and even begin to do well academically.

My roommate had made up his mind to pledge Sigma Chi, one of the most prestigious fraternities on campus. Not aware of how difficult it would be to get into such a fraternity, I decided I would pledge Sigma Chi as well. My roommate put on a blue blazer, gray slacks, and brown oxfords. I only had a pair of gray chinos, white socks, and penny loafers. He shaved and then slathered on a great-smelling cologne. I didn't have a clue what cologne was. We walked together to fraternity circle looking like Mutt and Jeff. The broad front lawn and the imposing four-columned stone house of Sigma Chi beckoned us.

My roommate and I couldn't have presented a greater contrast. He was suave and cool. I was a country hick, probably looking a lot like Sheldon did when I first met him at the waltz lessons. The brothers at Sigma Chi had no trouble deciding between my roommate and me. I wasn't even invited into the foyer of the house: I was turned down at the front door. In shock, I walked alone across fraternity circle to Beta Theta Phi. Same result. Then Sigma Alpha Epsilon. Then all the rest of the houses. I was turned down every time. Once again I felt utterly rejected.

From that day forward, I became a recluse. I wrote my parents every day and hung on every word of the letters they wrote back. Because parties at Denison largely revolved around the school's fraternities and sororities, my social life was nonexistent, and my grades continued to suffer. The only bright spot in life was my friendship with a sophomore named John Barrett, who did his best to make me feel that at least one person cared.

Matters came to a head in mid-October. A big freshman mixer featuring a well-known rock-and-roll band was being held in Livingston Gym. John encouraged me to go, saying I needed to get out of the dorm, but when I got there, I almost instantly regretted my decision. Apparently, it had been decided beforehand that pledges from each fraternity would link up with pledges from a sister sorority. Consequently, independents like me had no place to hang out. Worse, all the dancing was done by these pairs. I just stood in the door of the gym, hands in my pockets, watching the others having fun and wishing I could be a part of the action.

At 8 P.M. I went back to Smith Hall. I was the only person in the entire dorm. I sat on my bed crying, feeling like a complete loser. I then called my parents and told them, just like Sheldon recently did, that I wanted to come home. They were crushed.

The music in the Great Hall has picked up. I snap out of this bad daydream as Susan pulls me back up on the stage. Having failed with Sara, I try to do the swing with my wife, but I make a mess of it. Susan is a much better dancer than I am, so I finally give up. As I do this, the feeling of peace and happiness I experienced at seminar floods back.

Here I am, in a room full of young people, having a great time. So are my friends. There's Victoria, dancing with a young man across the room. She seems so shy in seminar, but here she is, whooping it up with the best of them. She gives me an uncharacteristic wink of recognition. There's Don across the room, the junior who gave me the tour during freshman orientation. He gives me a thumbs-up just before he dips his partner. I guess that a thumbs-up is just Don's way of greeting you. I see Morgan from my seminar sitting with Charles from my boat, probably engaged in deep philosophical conversation. Whether in sports, around the seminar table, or at a Waltz Party, everyone at St. John's fits in. Even an over-the-hill intellectual like me.

. . .

Melanoma is a disease that is always with you. Once it metastasizes, as it did with me, it can be deadly. And even if you are one of the fortunate few to go into long-term remission, it can hibernate and come back later. Researchers at Johns Hopkins and elsewhere are working on a vaccine that might one day prevent melanoma from recurring, but until this vaccine is developed or another treatment is discovered, I must always live with a monkey on my back. Am I through with this terrible disease? Or will it come back again?

This uncertainty has taken a toll. Every time I cough I wonder whether the melanoma has returned to my lungs. Whenever I see spots, I think that the melanoma has gone to my eyes. Ocular melanoma is not good. I also must live with numbness in my toes and fingers and ringing in my ears, probably a result of the Cisplatin I was also treated with. And who knows what causes the occasional sharp pains that travel up and down the side of my face, sometimes causing intolerable headaches.

To ensure that the melanoma hasn't come back, I must have

a CT scan every three months. In the beginning, the anxiety I experienced while waiting for the results was almost unbearable. Now, after having gone through the procedure more than a dozen times, they have become almost routine.

It's that time again, and so I must take two days off to get my scan done in Virginia and then return north to see my doctor at Johns Hopkins in Baltimore. I am feeling a deep sense of guilt, however, as I tell the coach that I will have to take a brief break from crew practice. I'm a member of a team now. The boathouse is my family, and my crewmates are like brothers. Am I letting them all down? Will the coach cut me from my boat? It's interesting to me how the matters that concerned me before this sabbatical—a balanced budget, enrollment figures, endowment returns—have been replaced with whether or not I will race at Occoquan next weekend with a boatload of teenagers.

"That's okay, Roger," Mr. Pickens says with feeling. "We'll miss you. Good luck."

I make the two-hour drive back to Ashland, getting to my house by noon. I stop by my office, pick up a mountain of memos, magazines, and junk mail that have been accumulating on my desk, greet people I see in Peele Hall, Randolph-Macon's administration building, and then go home to eat lunch and do some reading. I am behind in Plato's *Republic*. Nothing—certainly not the business of a college president—is going to interfere with my reading assignment.

The Randolph-Macon trustees meet this weekend, and were I not on sabbatical, I would be involved in a whirlwind of committee meetings and last-minute preparations for the board meeting. But I give the upcoming board meeting only a fleeting thought. My sabbatical at St. John's has taken hold, and I really feel like a student, not a college administrator. It's a good feeling, but I know it is only temporary. But right now, all I want to do is get through my medical tests and go back to St. John's.

I curl up on my bed with the TV remote in one hand and a cold beer in the other. I have two choices: either watch the World Series or finish the *Republic.* Plato wins out. Seduced by the knowledge that I will not have to wake up at 5 A.M., I fall asleep with the book open on my chest.

Morning comes quickly. It is still dark outside. Half asleep, and thinking that I am at my house on Franklin Street, I fumble for the clock radio, but I can't find it. I reach over to touch Susan. She isn't there either. I fall back on my pillow, confused. In my mind's eye I am back in Annapolis, where every morning I get out of bed, let the dog out to do her morning business, pull on my jogging shorts, sweatshirt, and nylon overalls—quietly, so as not to wake up Susan—and leave for the boathouse. But in reality, I'm alone in my house in Ashland, Virginia.

The alarm suddenly goes off. It's 6 A.M. Reality has set in, and I know where I am now. But as I brush my teeth, I imagine Mr. Pickens. He is lecturing the crew about some aspect of rowing. When he finishes, he is instructing them to pull their shells off the rack. "Let the women's eight go first," he is saying. But as this vision unfolds, I am not in the picture. Someone has replaced me in the *Harriet Higgins Warren.*

This thought causes me to become fully awake, wishing I were in Annapolis, not here in Ashland. I have actually become homesick for my new community. I want to get back to St. John's as quickly as I can.

I drive out to Regional Memorial Hospital in Mechanicsville, where the melanoma tumor was discovered four years ago, arriving just before my 7:30 A.M. appointment. I register and walk into the waiting room.

As I finish off the second pint of a disgusting barium solution in preparation for the CT scan that will soon be performed, I imagine my team rowing back to the boathouse after another tie race.

I am led to the CT room, where I begin to worry, although not about the cancer reappearing. What has me preoccupied is whether Coach will allow me to rejoin the team after missing two practices. I might not get to race at Occoquan.

. . .

I needn't have been concerned. When I return to practice the next morning, Mr. Pickens assigns me my regular seat in the *Harriet Higgins Warren*. But, as I soon discover, even two days' absence has its consequences.

Maia is still out sick, so Joe is again coxing. He tells us as we carry our shell out of the boathouse that he just put Mary on notice that our boat is going to "take the ladies down" in today's time trials. When he says this, the guys are yelling in unison, "Yeah! Yeah! Yeah!" As we approach the Occoquan race, my boat is getting pumped. They want to win.

As we row through College Creek toward the Severn, Joe says, "I'm going to make you guys row so hard this morning, that your ass will become joined to your neck. When you walk down Main Street in Annapolis, people are going to ask you, 'Why is your ass joined to your neck?' Just kidding, guys."

As he says this, a double suddenly rams into our stern. Joe stops his commentary and starts a yelling match with the two victims of the collision.

"You guys are both tools. Are you blind or something?"

"Your mother sucks wind, Joe."

"Your mother's a dweeb," Joe replies, without missing a beat.

Joe isn't completely to blame. It's dark, and the duo just didn't see us. But then again, because he was talking, Joe wasn't focused on the river, just like the other day.

We work on our form as we row up the Severn toward our starting point for the time trials. The crew in my boat are now talking among themselves. They don't just want to skunk the women's novice eight; they want to register the fastest time on the river.

Halfway toward the starting point, while we are doing Lady Margarets, Joe starts talking about Phoenician sailors. "You know, don't you, that the Phoenicians were the fastest rowers?"

"Yeah, we know that," Thom says, as though he wished Joe would just shut up and focus on being cox.

"And do you know why?"

No one answers.

"Because they had nubile Phoenician women to row home to."

I find this piece of information fascinating until, off to port, I hear Coach yelling at me from the skiff, "You're not focused, Roger. *Snap* those legs down. *Square* the oar. *Drop* the blade." Mr. Pickens is wrong. I am focused. I'm just focused on the wrong thing.

We are now at the starting point. Charlie suggests that to show that we are men, we race with our shirts off. "Yeah! Yeah! Yeah!" everyone shouts again, except me. It's very cold this early in the morning, and with part of my left lung missing, I can't afford to get pneumonia. Indeed, one of my fears as winter approaches and the temperature drops on the river is that I might experience respiratory problems. So I decide to do the St. John's thing and be a nonconformist. Everyone except me takes off his shirt. We must be a vision to behold: eight bare-chested teenagers and an old man bundled up in his hooded sweatshirt.

We lurch forward when Mr. Pickens gives us the command to start. Our shell is fueled by raw testosterone. The guys think they can win by brute force.

The boat seems unbalanced to me, and I have a difficult time pulling my oar out of the water at the release. I'm reminded of the two crabs I caught earlier in the season, and I fear the same thing might happen again.

About three minutes into the race, Charlie yells back at me, "For god's sake, Roger, get your blade out of the water." But I can't. The boat is listing too far to port. I regain my composure.

We continue to clip along at a rate that it is hard to imagine we can sustain considering that we are still a long distance from the Naval Academy Bridge and the seawall. In the past we would be rowing hard at this point, but not *this* hard. I am beginning to gasp for air, and sweat is pouring down my face. But just as I begin to wonder whether I can finish the race, Joe yells, "Weigh enough."

"How can this be?" I wonder, since we haven't yet reached the seawall. We haven't even reached the Naval Academy Bridge.

Finally I realize that the terminus for this race is a flagpole on Horseshoe Point, about 1,000 meters short of our normal ending point, and that we just passed over the finish line. Apparently, while I was in Virginia getting my CT scan, the team had been working on their speed by racing this shorter course. Everyone in the boat but me, then, knew where the finish line would be.

Still, I am relieved. My rowing wasn't great, but at least we beat the women's eight, making good on Joe's prediction. Unfortunately, we didn't win the overall race, and thus a necktie. I sense disappointment in the boat. And then it happens.

As we row into College Creek and back to the boathouse, isaac taps me on the back. "Roger, you really need to row better. You are slowing us down. We'll never win at Occoquan."

This penetrating comment really hurts. How would you feel if you were a college president with umpteen academic degrees (not to mention a very healthy ego) being told by a teenager who hasn't even made it through the first semester of freshman year that you were a failure? Not great. And how would you feel knowing that this kid is absolutely right? Even worse. I am Goliath, and this kid is David, and he has just shot me right between the eyes with just a few pointed words, totally deflating my grand presidential ego in the process.

Isaac's comment gives me pause. But being a bit more objective than the students (I suppose because I really *am* an adult), I find it somewhat ironic that what was supposed to be just a lot of fun has suddenly become a desire to win at all costs. These may be St. John's students, but they are also normal American teenagers. And American teenagers, of the male variety at least, want to "kick butt"—to use their term—whenever they're placed in a competitive situation. So, if I'm going to stay in the game, I'm going to have to desire the same thing and get with the program. But I still won't take my shirt off.

As we row into College Creek on our way back to the boathouse, Joe settles back into his normal chatter. "Do you like the cocoa they serve in the dining hall?" he asks nobody in particular. "I like it, but I like Irish coffee better, especially without the coffee." "Did you see the World Series last night? Well, I saw parts of it. Let me tell you about it . . ."

.   .   .

I'm in the bookstore again, this time looking for a good translation of Thucydides' *Peloponnesian War,* which our seminar will soon be reading. Thucydides, another historian, was a contemporary of Herodotus, of whom he was often critical. It will be fun to read another historian.

As I'm leafing through the several different translations available, Shannon joins me. I have not seen her since she shared with me her tale of woe.

"Looking for a translation of Thucydides?" I ask her.

"Yeah. Got to get a head start on it," she replies. Shannon is looking much brighter than the last time I saw her. She has given up the mod look—her hair is back to its natural color and the silver ring in her navel has disappeared—and is dressed more like a normal Johnnie, if there is such a thing.

"Got a minute?" she asks after checking out a couple of translations. "I need to tell you what's happened since we last talked."

"Sure," I respond. "Let's grab a cup of coffee." My caffeine addiction has reached the point where I am now willing to drink the coffee Don thought so terrible.

We both abandon our quest to find a translation of Thucydides and walk the short distance to the Coffee Shop. I am worried about what Shannon is going to tell me.

"Well, things are really looking up," Shannon says as I pay for our coffee and we take a seat in my regular spot. "I took your advice and went to the health center. They put me in touch with a therapist, and she has been wonderful. I really appreciate what you did for me."

"I really didn't do that much, Shannon," I say, relieved that she seems to have turned things around. "How did your sister make out?"

"Oh, Danielle's fine. She's not living at home anymore. She got a job as a waitress in a local restaurant, and I helped her find a place to live. My parents aren't happy with the situation, but I think it's better for everyone. Danielle's almost eighteen, and since she isn't going to college, at least not right away, she's got to make it on her own at some point. Might as well be now."

"That's great," I say as I sip my coffee.

"But there's more," Shannon says. "Right after I saw you, I went into a deep depression. I didn't think I was going to make it. But my roommate was really there for me. She saw that I was in pain. She walked over to the health center with me, and she has just been really supportive. And so have my other friends. It's just amazing to me, Mr. Martin, that all these people who I didn't even know before I came to St. John's would become my best friends. We're together all the time."

Shannon is talking a mile a minute, and it's clear she feels pretty good about what she has been able to accomplish. I'm feeling pretty good as well. When I first met her, I thought Shannon was a lost soul, but now I see a completely different person. I also see how important the St. John's community has become for her. And I remember how important community eventually became for me after a very rough start at Denison.

I, too, was wounded and feeling sorry for myself when I decided to drop out of college following the episode at Livingston Gym. But, like Shannon, I discovered that there were people who genuinely cared for me and who made the remaining months of my freshman year, if not enjoyable, at least tolerable. I just wish I had met them earlier. In addition to my friend John, I remember an older student who had been in the army before going to college; he helped me to see that these little setbacks in life were really small fish compared to the struggles endured by many people who can't afford a college education. He gave me a completely different perspective on my life. And I remember the dean of students, a big teddy bear of a man who spent hours trying to help me deal with my social and academic demons so that perhaps I could salvage the rest of my freshman year. Even though I was homesick, not doing well academically, and struggling to cope with my immaturity, there was still a small community at Denison that became everything to me until I finally returned home at the end of spring semester. Had I a bit more character and maturity, perhaps I would have stayed the course at Denison.

Shannon and I talk like this for another half hour. She then tells me that she has a meeting with one of her tutors in fifteen minutes, which reminds me that I was supposed to meet Susan ten minutes ago to attend a pizza party with the crew team.

"I am really happy for you, Shannon," I say as we get up to leave. "You seem to have sorted things out."

She smiles at me. "Since you've given me such great advice, Mr. Martin, I have some for you," she says.

"What's that, Shannon?"

"Don't buy the Charles Smith translation of *The Peloponnesian War*. It really sucks."

. . .

I rush over to the new dorm. As I am jogging across the playing fields I spot Susan parking the car, so we enter the dorm's lounge together.

The last time we attended one of these functions, the evening of the hurricane, we felt somewhat out of place. This time we feel much more as if we belong, despite my setback yesterday with Isaac. Sure, I am a whole lot older than they are, but our differences in age and status matter little. No longer are we novices and grizzled veterans, freshmen and seniors, but instead we are members of a team, each with a particular purpose and function. We are a community, and I have earned a place in this community through perseverance and hard work.

As we wait for the pizza to be served, I think about Plato's discussion of the ideal city. In particular, I'm reminded of Sebastian's comments in seminar the other day when we were talking about the Guardians. It was Sebastian who pointed out that if the farmers don't farm, the Guardians starve. Everyone in the republic is important. As I observe the young men on my team, I can see Sebasian's point.

Over there, next to the panoramic window, is Joe, probably regaling some of his teammates with his pop philosophy and movie reviews. In the boat, he is our wannabe philosopher-king and source of entertainment. But if it weren't for our stroke, Thom, who is in the kitchen helping slice the pizza, we would all row out of sync. And if it weren't for David, sitting on the couch talking to Victoria, I wouldn't know what to do when the cox box is on the fritz. And Isaac, who is just entering the room with Charlie, has become my conscience. He reminds me that if I row badly, our whole boat will suffer. The better we work together, the more likely we will achieve the perfection Plato describes. In our case, this means winning races, and especially doing well at Occoquan.

We eat our pizza and the evening passes quickly. Just before the party ends, a group of us speculate on the length of the Occoquan course. Is it 2,000, 5,000, or 6,000 meters? Just like at the Severn Chase, no one seems to know. After yesterday's incident, I realize that I need to know the length of the race in advance so that I can pace myself. As soon as I get home I look up "Head of the Occoquan" on the Internet, where I find a map of the course. It is very different from the straight course we have been rowing on the Severn. The course, on a reservoir in northern Virginia, follows a series of loops and turns, but there is no indication of where the race begins and ends. I note the average times for past races, about nineteen minutes for novice eights. But is this over a 5,000- or a 6,000-meter course?

I make a mental note of this information and begin to psyche myself up for the big event.

. . .

It's the eve of the Head of the Occoquan. Today will be the dress rehearsal for what happens tomorrow. To my utter surprise and delight, I see Maia, our cox, when I arrive at the boathouse. She looks a bit tired, but she seems to be herself again. She will once again cox the *Harriet Higgins Warren.*

Mr. Pickens announces that in preparation for tomorrow's race we will do assorted drills, ending with a 5,000-meter tie race. "Just relax and enjoy yourselves," is the unlikely advice he gives us at the end of his peroration. *None* of us are just enjoying ourselves. We are all scared witless.

This morning we're all alone on the Severn, but according to the scuttlebutt going around, thousands of people will be watching us from the banks of the Occoquan tomorrow. There will be no more solitary practices witnessed only by our coach and a few watermen in their crab boats. Tomorrow is show time. And I have to wonder: Will I have the endurance to complete the race? Will I be an embarrassment to myself and to my crew? Will I catch a crab?

We take the *Harriet Higgins Warren* off the storage rack and carry her down to the dock. Maia's resolute commands boost our confidence. Not only is she a good cox, but she has also raced at Occoquan herself and knows the course well.

We glide out of College Creek rowing with only one arm. This exercise is supposed to isolate the function of the outboard arm. Once we make the turn at the seawall and start rowing up-river, we row very slowly, perhaps at a rate of eighteen strokes per minute, while focusing on our form. I try to concentrate on four things: watching Thom at stroke, so that my blade enters and exits the water exactly when his does; keeping my oar handle loose in my hands when I feather so as not to catch a crab; letting the oar drop in the water at the catch; and springing with my legs off the footboards and then pulling my oar handle toward my chest during the drive. I come up with a mantra: "Watch Thom. Feather lightly. Watch Thom. Drop oar in water. Watch Thom. Thrust legs."

We slowly row past the Route 50 Bridge. As we approach the starting point of our race, Charles's oarlock starts making a strange popping sound. This is not good. One of the worst things that can happen during a race is for the hardware that fastens the riggers to the gunwales of the boat to lose their fasteners and fall off. Coach motors over in his skiff and checks out the problem. He pulls out a wrench from the tool chest in the skiff's bow and tightens the riggers, but the popping sounds persist. Finally, Coach asks Charles to change places with Charlie, and the sound mysteriously goes away. The race is on.

Maia is the ultimate cox and a voice of calm under pressure. In the past we have jumped out of these starts with raw energy, causing us to row out of concert. Maia won't allow this to happen. "Okay, you guys, suppress your male macho urges," she tells us. I recall our seminar's discussion of the *Iliad,* when the guys supported an approach to conflict resolution that was more physical than that of the women, an approach that was of questionable effectiveness even thousands of years ago. "Let's start out smooth, get our cadence, and then row like pros so we can win this race." I miss Joe's jokes and stories, but as the race approaches, I appreciate Maia's confidence and steadiness.

We're lined up to begin the race. Coach announces that we will row the entire distance back to the seawall at a racing rate of twenty-eight strokes per minute, with intermittent power tens, and then go all out to the finish line. A chill runs up and down my spine and I go into deep prayer: "Lord, don't let me fail." Soon we're off.

As I row, I notice that I am leaning far to the starboard side of the boat. I'm also slipping on my seat. I try to compensate by sitting up straight. This helps a little, but not much. I put this concern out of my head and just focus on the race, repeating to myself my mantra: "Watch Thom. Feather lightly. Watch Thom. Drop oar in water. Watch Thom. Thrust legs."

Throughout the race my mind is a blur, and all I can hear is the click of the oarlocks. I get into a cadence and just row the best I can. Click, click, click. Pull. Click, click, click. Pull. Click, click, click. Pull. I don't even remember passing under the Naval Academy Bridge, though I can recall seeing Henry out of the corner of my eye, still rowing in a solitary scull. We steam past him.

Suddenly, to my left I see the first of the eight floodlights on the Naval Academy seawall, a welcome sight. We have been rowing fairly constantly at a pace of twenty-eight strokes per minute. All of us are absolutely spent. Maia is now yelling encouragement. She tells us to pour it on.

This last command is a big mistake. Testosterone, our worst enemy, takes over. Our pace is now too fast, and the boat is thrown badly off-kilter, and it's too late to correct ourselves. We pass over the finish line, but once again, we are not in first place.

Back in the boathouse we go through the traditional Friday necktie award ceremony. Mr. Pickens announces the times. Ours was twenty-three minutes flat. Knowing from my research the other night that the normal time at Occoquan for a novice men's eight is eighteen to twenty minutes, our time seems slow to me. On the other hand, I'm still not sure how long the course at Occoquan is.

Coach next tells us that we must decide what our uniform will be for tomorrow's big race. Charlie yells out from the back of the boathouse, "Painted faces and no shirts!" But Dan, an upperclassman who has rowed at Occoquan before, reminds everyone that shirts are required by the race committee, so Coach puts a nix on that suggestion. I am relieved to know that

I won't have to imitate what I often see freshmen do at major athletic events, namely, make total asses of themselves in front of large crowds of people. I am reminded again that I'm not really a freshman.

Thom suggests that we all buy black St. John's T-shirts, which are available in the college bookstore. This is a controversial decision, since Johnnies hate to wear anything that resembles a uniform.

As I am about to leave, Mike, the assistant coach, beckons me to join him at the back of the boathouse.

"Roger," he says, "you seem really nervous."

"Mike, I'm just not rowing well," I confess, thankful for an understanding person who will listen to my frustrations. "I'm leaning to the starboard, and I think I'm slowing my boat down."

"I've noticed that as well," he responds. "Come over here and lie on your back." I follow Mike's instructions.

"Okay," Mike says, "now pull up your knees to your chest." When I do this, my head automatically rises from the floor.

"I think I know what the problem is. Your lower spine seems to be fused, probably from age, and so it acts like the runners on a rocking chair." As Mike says this, I recall my first day of rowing in the barge, when my lack of flexibility caused me to collide with Sara. Mike then suggests some exercises I might do to become a bit more limber.

Ironically, I am greatly relieved. No one wants to be told that their spine lacks flexibility or that they are getting old, but knowing that my rowing style is directly related to a physical defect in my back and not to a lack of rowing skill is a comfort. At my age, understanding things like this is very important.

As I am about to leave the boathouse, Mr. Pickens approaches me. He puts both of his hands squarely on my shoulders and looks straight at me with those no-nonsense, piercing eyes. "You'll do fine, Roger. Just relax and enjoy yourself." He, too, has detected my concern and is responding like the excellent coach he is.

I leave the boathouse with Thom, who has been making last-minute adjustments to our rigging. "I don't know about you," he says, "but I almost lost it today." I commiserate with him. It's good to know that at least one other member of our boat is also struggling.

"Roger, how long will you be at St. John's?" he asks me.

"Until December 17th," I reply.

"What then?"

"I return to my college."

"What college?" Thom asks.

"Randolph-Macon in Virginia," I say.

"What do you do there?"

"I'm president."

"No kidding. That's awesome."

"Who did you think I was?" I ask Thom. "I thought everyone knew I was a college president."

Thom pauses so he can ponder how to diplomatically answer this last question. And then, with a twinkle in his eye, he says, "Oh, some not-too-bright older guy desperately trying to get a college degree." We both laugh.

·　·　·

The great day has arrived. Last night, just before going to bed, I called Kate for some last-minute advice. I told her about my nervousness, about my lack of flexibility, about how I lean away from the oar. She calmed me down and said, echoing Coach Pickens, "Dad, just enjoy the race. You'll do fine."

I plant a big kiss on Susan's cheek (she and her mother will join me at Occoquan later in the day), say goodbye to our dog, Angel, who has shared these early mornings with me, pack my bags, and drive up Franklin Street to the boathouse.

Almost everyone has assembled by the time I arrive. It's still dark, and the trailer that will carry our shells is poised to leave, looking like some kind of sea monster straight out of Jules Verne.

Our job this morning is simply to dismantle the riggings on the shells, wash down the hulls, and then load the shells onto the trailer. It's amazing to see the team working together in almost perfect unison. There is very little talk. There doesn't need to be. We all know what to do.

When this task has been accomplished, Mr. Pickens calls us to the back of the boathouse for a powwow. This will be his last pep talk.

For many in the boathouse, this is just another race, another athletic event like the many they participated in throughout high school. But for me this race marks a milestone. Occoquan will be the last time I will compete in an athletic contest. I thought the last time was thirty-six years ago, when I ended my collegiate rugby career. But my fantasy of competing one last time will come true tomorrow, and I am *really* nervous. I'm nervous not only because I might disappoint myself, but, more importantly, because I might ruin the race for my teammates. My sabbatical was originally meant to be just for me, an experience that I would enjoy doing but that otherwise would not affect anyone else, except perhaps Susan and Angel. But my sabbatical has taken on an unexpected dimension. I am a member of a team of young student athletes, and so if I fail, I affect others. Just like in Plato's *Republic,* my actions could mean the success or failure of the entire community.

"Okay, listen up. Are you all ready for the Festival of St. Occoquan?" Coach asks the assembled group. They all nod their assent, laughing at the funny name he has made up for this event.

"Good. Now, I have some important things to say. First, I want to commend all of you for the time and energy you have put into this sport. No matter how well you perform this afternoon, you should all feel a great sense of accomplishment." He then gives us some startling figures.

"Those of you who are the grizzled veterans have put in ninety hours of practice, the novices eighty. And you've done this while being students in an incredibly demanding academic program. Few college students who will be competing at Occoquan this afternoon have had to balance the requirements of study and classes with the demands of practice. You have done well. You are ready to race. You have achieved perfection. *I declare this boathouse a republic!*"

Now, what Coach has just said would mean little to the outside observer, but he knows that in their seminars the freshmen are nearing the end of Plato's *Republic,* a book that all the upperclassmen have read as well. His comment brings to mind Socrates' description of the perfect city-state and, by inference, the perfect citizen. Socrates says that in order for a city to be just, there must be leaders and common citizens, all of them doing their part for the good of the whole. When we started this process back in early September, we were forty individuals who didn't row very well together. Sometimes we didn't show up for practice. Often we were more focused on our individual needs and aspirations than on the team, or we were just overwhelmed with schoolwork. But this morning, we are a community. Not only are we rowing much better, but we also care about one another. And there is a spirit—a team spirit—that is unparalleled. Maybe Coach Pickens has exaggerated. We are obviously far from perfect. But we really are a sort of republic, and everyone understands exactly what Coach has just said.

"Okay, my friends. Now let's enjoy the race." We leave the boathouse for the van and cars that will carry us one hour south to the Occoquan Reservoir.

CHAPTER 8

Victory

I am driving south, down Route 95, to the Head of the Occoquan with Susan. The woman in my car is not my wife, but another person named Susan who is a student at the Graduate
Institute. Like my friend Sara, Susan is a tiny woman who rows
in the women's novice eight. A graduate of a small college in
Florida, Susan came to St. John's to broaden her intellectual
horizons and prepare to pursue a PhD somewhere else. We
carry on a lively conversation about theology and the Greek
classics. I am glad I am driving with Susan, because our chatter
keeps my mind off what is going to happen in only a couple of
hours.

Following close behind Mr. Pickens, who is towing a trailer
piled high with our shells, we arrive in no time at Sandy Run
Regional Park, about twenty-five miles south of Washington,
D.C. Usually this is a pleasant wooded park surrounding the
Occoquan Reservoir, but this morning it is an absolute mad-
house. I later learn that several thousand people are present for

this event, including six hundred college students who are competing in a variety of races involving eights, fours, doubles, and single sculls. As consequence, all the trailers, vans, and charter buses, not to mention private cars like my own, converging on the park create an enormous traffic jam. I have attended races like this one before, mostly in New England, where I watched Kate compete, but most of my teammates haven't, and I can only imagine their wonder at seeing this spectacle. Susan, the graduate student, and I park in an area overlooking the reservoir and rejoin our team.

I have never been to Sandy Run before, though I have driven past it many times on trips between Ashland and Washington, D.C. The site is rather majestic. The area where the trailers and vans are parked is high on a hill overlooking the tree-lined reservoir, which is three hundred feet or more below us. Off in the distance, to the west, I can see part of our racecourse. Single sculls are leaving the staging area just below and rowing upstream toward the starting point, which is out of sight from where I stand. The view from this eagle's perch in the parking area can only be described as intimidating. For the last leg of our race, my team and I will have to row as far as we can currently see, which is only to the first turn in the reservoir. Since we cannot see the rest of the course, its distance can only be imagined. As the single sculls leaving for their race make their first turn to the right at the end of this long finger of water, they look like a string of tiny ants. Soon we can't see them at all. For all I know they have been gobbled up by the man-eating monster Scylla.

When an event is announced over the loudspeaker near the spectator's stand, directly across from the finish line, the competitors must carry their shells down a long gravel path to one of several docks at the water's edge. This way twenty or so shells can be launched into the Occoquan in a matter of minutes. If a race weren't taking place, this path would look like a pretty country road leading down to an equally pretty body of water, but today groups of students are huddled on each side of the path next to trailers that are piled high with almost every kind of racing boat imaginable.

The trailers themselves are decorated with the banners of the competing colleges and universities. To my right I see West Point's trailer, in front of which a grand picnic table has been assembled for team members and their families. West Point, as one might expect, does not have a nationally ranked crew like the Naval Academy, so Army races in regional events like this one. The Naval Academy competes at the national level, against the likes of Yale and Harvard. Directly across the path is a large area for Johns Hopkins University, and next to them is the University of Maryland. St. John's area is shared with its sister Maryland school, Washington College.

Between this phalanx of trailers and crews are eights and fours and single sculls being portaged down to the reservoir and the staging area, while other shells are being carried in the opposite direction after their races. Crowds of people are milling around, making us all feel as though there were a gigantic tailgate party taking place. It is

Our race is scheduled for 11 A.M., so I have some time to wander around with my wife and Marjorie, my mother-in-law, both of whom have just arrived. As we walk down toward the staging area at the base of the hill, I overhear a coach admonishing a group of women. They are from a large university that will soon be competing in a varsity women's eight. "You didn't get a medal last year, girls. It was a real embarrassment to me personally, and to the university. So are you going to screw up again this year or win something?" I can't hear the rest of this speech as we continue to walk down the path, but the expression on the faces of the crew is etched in my memory. They are not happy campers. I feel sorry for this team, since rowing is probably a burden for them.

It's getting close to launch time, so we wander back up to the parking area and the St. John's trailer. The students are sitting on the ground eating energy bars and oranges. There isn't a whole lot of chatter, and I sense that everyone is somewhat intimidated by the spectacle going on around them. Off to the side of the trailer, however, I notice that Matt, a senior and one of the captains of the team, is reading an essay by Thomas Mann for his senior preceptorial. He rows in the varsity quad, and his race isn't until this afternoon, so Matt is using this downtime to his advantage. The image of Matt reading next to the trailer is also etched in my mind. St. John's, as Mr. Pickens reminded us earlier, is an academic institution first. Nothing, not even Occoquan, is more important than Thomas Mann.

As we wait for our first call, I again wonder how long the course is. As happened at the Severn Chase, Coach has forgotten to give us this information—or, more likely, I wasn't paying attention. I ask Maia, who rowed here when she was in high school. "I think it's 6,000 meters," she says, "but I'm not sure."

"You're kidding," responds David, who has been listening in on our conversation. "We'll never make it."

David is as nervous as I am about the distance we are expected to row, so I decide to take matters into my own hands. I want to know exactly how long the race is so that I can pace myself. Coach is standing next to the trailer, helping to unload the oars. I screw up my courage and ask him how long we will row. "Five thousand meters," he tersely says, "just like you rowed yesterday." I pass the word on to Maia and my teammates.

While I have Maia's attention, I tell her that I found a map of the Occoquan racecourse on the Internet, which indicated that off to one side of the final stretch there is a group of rocks decorated with graffiti, probably the artwork of generations of high school and college students who have raced here. "By my calculation these rocks are about 500 meters from the finish line," I tell her, "about the same distance from the first to the last floodlight on the Naval Academy seawall. When we reach them," I continue, "why don't you tell us, as you always do when we race on the Severn that we are at the Naval Academy seawall? This will give us confidence to end the race strong."

Maia gives me an odd look, which seems to say, "Have you gone ballistic, Roger?" but she says nothing. I think she is nervous, just like the rest of us.

First call for the men's novice eights is heard over the loudspeaker. All nine of us assemble next to the *Harriet Higgins Warren* and on Maia's command lift it off the trailer and begin to walk it down the path toward the launch area. There is a monumental traffic jam as nineteen novice eights all head down the hill but are met at the halfway point by an equal number of fours heading back up after finishing their race.

We finally make it to the dock at the bottom of the hill. The area reminds me of Chicago's O'Hare airport at about 11 A.M. on a weekday morning, when hundreds of planes are trying to take off and land at the same time. Absolute chaos.

Just before we launch our boat into the water, an official pins a placard with the number 110 on Maia's back. This will be the number of our boat. Four other teams just behind us on the long dock drop their boats into the water as we do. And there we are: a team of eight men and one woman, all in black St. John's T-shirts except for Charlie, who, in keeping with St. John's tradition of nonconformity, has chosen to wear a bright yellow sweatshirt instead.

On Maia's command we begin rowing toward the starting point of the race, which, as I now know, is 5,000 meters away, through a labyrinth of bends and turns in the reservoir. At the moment, the finish line and the spectator's area, where there are crowds cheering on a race that is about to end, are in full view as we row away. I'm sure my teammates are thinking about how happy they will be when we get back down to this part of the racecourse and cross the finish line. Off to my right I now see the graffitied rocks indicated on the map. I wonder whether Maia has seen them as well.

Soon we see single sculls appearing from around the bend. These are the little ants I saw from the hilltop, when they were rowing toward the starting point. Now they are on the last leg of their race. David, who is always turning around in his seat so that he can see where we are going, says excitedly, "I can see Henry. I can see Henry. Look to the right. Do you see him?" We all crane our necks so that we can watch Henry rowing toward the finish line.

"Okay, guys," Maia, ever the leader, says. "On the count of three yell, 'Go, Henry!' One, two, three." We all yell as Maia has instructed us. We can see the pain in Henry's face as he rows the last five hundred meters, and we hope that our cheers have given him some extra energy and encouragement to finish strong. But seeing Henry this way has also given us a glimpse of what we will be going through ourselves in just a few minutes.

We are now instructed by a judge in a skiff similar to the one Coach Pickens uses to row quickly to the other side of the reservoir and then to proceed up the left side, but at a faster clip than we have been rowing. Somehow we have fallen behind our competitors, and we must be at the starting line on time. Maia instructs us to row at a rate of twenty-four strokes per minute. We round a bend in the reservoir at this quick pace, and now we can no longer see the spectators' area or the finishing line, just woods and some beautiful mansions on both sides of the reservoir. But I'm getting tired, wondering whether I'm going to be exhausted before the race even begins.

We approach a second turn in the reservoir, slow down a bit, and then, at the urging of yet another judge, whose skiff is anchored in the middle of the course, we pick up our pace again. We are still behind schedule. Finally, after two more turns in the reservoir, we reach the starting line.

An armada of eights pops into view, all just sitting around waiting to begin the race. The scene reminds me of Herodotus's description of the 378 Greek ships converging on Salamis to do battle with Xerxes and the Persians, except instead of *triremes* and *pentekonters* representing the Corinthians, Megarians, Aeginetans, and Chalcidians, I see eight-man shells representing the likes of Bucknell, Virginia Tech, and American University.

We rest only for a minute, and then we are instructed by the head judge to quickly row to the starting point.

In the confusion of the moment, it's hard to tell whom we will be racing against. But soon I recognize the painted oars of two boats in our immediate vicinity. They are St. Mary's College, the number 109 boat, who will leave right ahead of us, and the University of Maryland, number 111, who will leave just behind. In a head race like this one, time from start to finish determines the winner, but you're also trying to pass the boats in front of you and *not* be passed by the boats immediately to the stern. That the University of Maryland will be starting just after us worries me. Maryland is a university of some 20,000 students, and while every novice who went out for crew at St. John's is rowing today, Maryland has probably been able to select only the very best of their novices for the boat we are now about to compete against.

Almost as soon as we approach the starting line we are signaled by the head judge to take off. No rest is afforded us. Maia has us start at a rate of twenty-six strokes per minute, and we are almost immediately off-kilter. The nervous energy that has been building up in these guys is released in one chaotic explosion of raw male energy. We will never win the race this way.

But I've got bigger fish to fry. Only thirty seconds into the race I notice that for some reason my seat can roll only halfway down the slide, which means that I cannot completely extend my legs on the drive. There seems to be a mechanical problem, and there is nothing I can do about it. And then, as I worry about this, I almost catch a crab.

Stay focused on Thom, I think to myself. Don't worry about the seat. I begin repeating my mantra: "Watch Thom. Feather lightly. Watch Thom. Drop oar in water. Watch Thom. Thrust legs."

I settle down and the other guys do as well. We are now rowing much better than we did at the start.

As we approach the first bend in the reservoir, Maia decides to pick up the pace. "In four, bring it up to twenty-eight," she shouts. We do as she orders, but I'm getting *really* tired, and we haven't even completed the first quarter of the race. Worse, I can see number 111, the University of Maryland, gaining on us.

Maia sees Maryland as well, and as we approach the second turn she brings the pace up to thirty strokes per minute and then almost immediately calls for a power ten. I'll never make it at this rate, I am thinking to myself. Thirty is what we do at the Naval Academy seawall on the Severn when we are *finishing* the race. We have only begun! I almost catch a second crab because I'm not dropping my oar into the water. It's going in sideways because of fatigue. I remember Coach's instructions—"*Snap* those legs down. *Square* the oar. *Drop* the blade"—and I start doing this as though I were on the Severn and Mr. Pickens were in the skiff right next to me, watching my every move.

I'm now in a state of semiconsciousness. I wonder whether I will collapse as we round the third bend. No, I can't let these guys down, I think. Watch Thom. Feather lightly. Watch Thom. Drop oar in water. Watch Thom. Thrust legs. *Don't give up.*

I can't see the University of Maryland team anymore. Perhaps the power ten Maia had us do a minute ago discouraged them. Of course, I can't see what is in front of us either, but Maia can. Just as I am recovering from the last power ten, she calls above the voices of the other coxes goading on their teams, telling us to increase our rate to thirty-six strokes per minute, something we have never done before. I'm pouring sweat, and my arms and legs are absolutely aching. For some reason I am thinking of

Thucydides' description in *The Peloponnesian War* of the Athenians and Syracusans rowing into battle with each other:

> For on both sides there was more than ample exhortation and shouting on the part of the coxswains, both as part of their work and in the rivalry of the moment.
>
> *(Thucydides* Peloponnesian War *7:70)*

As this imagery swirls through my feeble mind, I almost catch a crab for the third time, but I dig in as we round the last bend and head toward the finish.

"Okay, guys, we're at the Naval Academy seawall," I hear Maia yelling as the graffitied rocks appear in the periphery of my vision. We all know exactly what this means: we only have five hundred meters to go. We are almost at the end. Miraculously, all of us get a third wind, and we row like we have never rowed before. I'm again leaning well out to the starboard, and my seat is still stuck so that it slides only halfway, but I don't care anymore. I am rowing as hard as everyone else, accelerating my blade through the water on the drive to help give the boat extra speed.

I barely hear the shriek of a whistle deep in the inner recesses of my numb brain, but we continue to row. We are all on automatic. "We're over," Maia yells. "We did it!" The whistle finally registers. We all fall backward on one another like dominos, first Thom, then Robert, then all of us. We are spent. Done for. Totally exhausted. But at this moment I am praying, "Thank you, God, for keeping me going." My greatest fear was catching a crab, stopping the boat, and ruining it for everyone, but that didn't happen. I performed well. And Maia, with all of her good judgment and wisdom, has proven to be the true philosopher-king in our boat.

I tap Isaac on his foot to congratulate him. He is stretched out prone in the bow. "Thanks, Roger," he says, still out of breath. "You rowed really well today." David then turns around and shakes my hand.

"Do you know who came in behind us?" I ask him, still gasping for breath. David doesn't have a clue. "We held off number 111, the University of Maryland," I say, "and that's no small achievement."

As we drift with the current down the reservoir, the guys are regaining their composure. They have caught their breath and it is beginning to dawn on them what they have accomplished. Our final time was twenty minutes, thirty seconds, putting us near the back of the pack, but hardly last. Maryland, even though they didn't pass us, beat us by only six seconds. Meanwhile, we snookered several universities a whole lot larger than little St. John's. Not bad for a motley crew of Johnnies.

But for me, this is my swan song. Never again will I compete in an intercollegiate athletic event. This will be a memory that lasts forever.

. . .

Several weeks have passed since the great race. I was supposed to compete one last time, in a fun event on College Creek called the Ritter Cup, but two nights before the race I received a phone call from Randolph-Macon that my college's former basketball coach had passed away and that his memorial service would be taking place in Petersburg, Virginia, on the same weekend. I realize that my time as a freshman is coming to an end as I prematurely resume my presidential persona. Crew practice is over for me, and, as happened when my college rugby career ended,

I am feeling a real void in my life, even though I continue to attend freshman seminar and frequent the Coffee Shop.

My situation has changed in another way as well. A young reporter for the *Washington Post,* Daniel de Vise, got wind of my sabbatical project and just wrote a story in the national edition of his paper, which, when it was picked up by the Associated Press, got flashed around the globe. I have mixed feelings about this. Randolph-Macon and St. John's are getting incredible press coverage, but in the eyes of my classmates, I'm no longer just a college student.

The students at St. John's take my celebrity status and the visibility their college is now getting as a mixed blessing. They are proud of the fact that St. John's has purposefully avoided the hype of the notorious college beauty contests featured each year in magazines such as *US News and World Report* and the *Princeton Review,* and they are not used to the publicity that is now intruding upon their campus. "Has St. John's suddenly emerged from relative obscurity and found itself in good standing with the *many,* of all hideous fates?" a staff writer for the *Gadfly* wonders in print when, of all things, a camera crew from the *Today Show* appears on campus. And frankly, I share their concern. I did not mean for my sabbatical to become a media event. On the other hand, the students seem to take some pride that their college is being noticed by millions of people, including their parents.

I'm sitting alone now in the Coffee Shop, reflecting on the past couple of weeks and what has happened to me since I arrived at St. John's in August. As I do this, I notice that when they enter the room I am in, faculty acknowledge my presence as though I were some kind of visiting dignitary. Before the

Washington Post article I was almost entirely invisible to the faculty since I had taken great care to avoid them. Now that they know who I really am, I am treated with respectful deference. Worse, students are more reticent about coming over to chat with me. So I am sitting by myself, in my usual seat, deep in thought.

I am thinking back to August, when I participated in orientation, which now seems like ages ago. Back then I was an awkward older guy who was desperately trying to fit in, trying to make connections with my new classmates—but usually embarrassing myself in the process—and coping with the adolescent insecurities that had haunted me since my real freshman year. At least from Thom's perspective, I was a not-too-bright older guy not only trying to finally get a college education but, of all incredible things, also trying to be an athlete. I must have seemed pathetic to my classmates.

But by the time Occoquan happened, I had morphed into a proper student who, though still somewhat out of place both in seminar and in the boathouse, nevertheless had become a true member of this small college community. I had made friends, some of them fairly close. I had shown Isaac that I could row with a bunch of teenagers and, if not excel, at least not embarrass the boat. Most importantly, I had won a victory over self-doubt.

But also running through my mind is a persistent question from the reporters who have been interviewing me: "Come on, level with us, Roger. Why did you *really* do this?" To them, the idea of a sixty-one-year-old college president going back to college is somewhat wacky. Indeed, this is why they are covering my sabbatical in the media. They really cannot fathom why anyone in my position would do a zany thing like enrolling as a freshman and, most amazingly of all, entering an intercollegiate head race at Occoquan. Why did I do this? And what has this experience meant to me in larger terms? I find a clue, as you might expect, in Plato.

. . .

Seminar is reading Plato's three works that describe the last days of Socrates' life: the *Apology,* the *Crito,* and the *Phaedo.* Socrates has spent his entire life as a gadfly, trying to engage people in conversation and debate to discover for themselves what is just and beautiful, criticizing the society in which he lives, calling knaves and fools for what they really are, and arguing with politicians and orators who are full of themselves. Finally, those in power in Athens have had enough, and Socrates is arrested on trumped-up charges of "corrupting the young and not believing in the gods." He is thrown into jail and put on trial for his life.

In the *Apology,* the first of the three dialogues, Socrates defends himself before his peers in a court of law. Knowing Socrates from his previous works—*Meno, Gorgias,* and, most recently, the *Republic*—we fear he will not be very diplomatic when he defends himself against the charges. True to form, Socrates shows his accusers little mercy. He certainly doesn't help his cause when he tells them that he was called by the gods to be a nuisance and threatens that "I [will] never cease to rouse each and every one of you, to persuade and reproach you all day long and everywhere I find myself in your company" (Plato *Apology* 30e, 31a).

In the second dialogue, one of Socrates' followers—a man by

the name of Crito—tries to convince Socrates, who has been condemned to death, to escape from jail. Crito and his friends plan to bribe the guard, and all Socrates needs to do is agree to the plan. But Socrates is a man of honor and high moral principle and will have nothing to do with Crito's proposal, arguing that, as a citizen of Athens, he must obey its laws. He asks Crito, "Do you think it is possible for a city not to be destroyed if the verdicts of its courts have no force but are nullified and set at naught by private individuals?" (Plato *Crito* 50b).

The third and most powerful work in the trilogy is the *Phaedo,* in which Socrates, in the presence of his followers who are visiting him in jail, faces the fact that the end of his life is imminent. Socrates describes death in moving prose, arguing that the body is transitory and that only in death can wisdom and pure knowledge be obtained. In a moving speech, he tells his friends, "I want to make my argument before you . . . as to why I think that a man who has truly spent his life in philosophy is probably right to be of good cheer in the face of death and to be very hopeful that after death he will attain the greatest blessings yonder" (Plato *Phaedo* 63e–64a). Socrates has great faith. He is also fearless.

As Socrates swallows the hemlock that will take his life, he utters these mysterious words: "Crito, we owe a cock to Asclepius; make this offering to him and do not forget" (ibid. 118a).

My classmates are now trying to fathom how Socrates could get himself into such a pickle. They all agree that he is sometimes his own worst enemy and that his mode of enquiry, the so-called Socratic method of argument, more often than not turns people off.

"I don't think Socrates means to be malicious," Alyssa says.

"He really wants to help. But too often, he achieves the opposite effect and makes people really angry with him."

"That's right," Morgan adds. "Socrates is a self-appointed gadfly, and lots of people resent this."

"Socrates goes back into the cave," Sebastian says, drawing seminar back to the *Republic,* "and tries to convince the prisoners to leave. But they don't want to see the truth, and they end up resenting his good intentions."

"What, then, is philosophy?" Mrs. Kronsberg asks. She quickly adds, "Is philosophy the act of undermining everything and always turning the world upside down, as Socrates seems to be doing here?"

"It's showing people that when they think something is right it could be wrong," Emily answers.

"I disagree," Dan says, perhaps trying to play devil's advocate. "I don't think Socrates is really philosophizing. I think he is a busybody who should probably mind his own business."

"No way," Zach says, seeming quite offended by Dan's suggestion. "Socrates didn't initiate these dialogues. Other people did. He is *not* a busybody. He challenges these people's stupid assumptions. He *is* a philosopher."

"But isn't Socrates always going around trying to find out what people know?" Mrs. Kronsberg persists. "Might not this be irritating to people?"

"Yeah," Elizabeth agrees. "He is basically a nosy person."

"But the task of a philosopher *is* to be nosy," Garret objects. "Socrates is just doing his job." Is asking questions a job?

The seminar falls silent for a good two or three minutes. We all ponder in silence whether Socrates is philosophizing or whether he is just being a pain in the butt.

Is Asking questions a job?

I can tell when Mr. Holland is about to pose a question because he leans far forward over the table. He surveys the class. He puts his index fingers to his lips as though he were in prayer. Only then does he break the silence by changing the subject. We now focus on Socrates' impending death.

"What does 'practicing death' mean?" Mr. Holland asks.

"Practicing death means getting past *who* we are to *what* we are; that is, getting beyond the body," Garret responds.

"And only by getting beyond the body, when we die, can we really understand what true justice and good is," Justin adds.

"To be a true philosopher," Annie suggests, "one has to transcend the body."

Students around the table seem to be nodding their heads in agreement with this last exchange.

Mr. Holland resists this consensus view. "What is Socrates getting at with his last words to Crito? Do they have anything to do with the body?" He is referring to the mysterious passage "Crito, we owe a cock to Asclepius; make this offering to him and do not forget."

The class is silent again. Victoria, who is normally very quiet, then draws attention to a footnote in her text. "In my edition of *Phaedo,*" she says, "the translator says that a cock was sacrificed to Asclepius, the god of medicine, by sick people who had visited his temple, hoping that by doing so they would get well again. Perhaps Socrates is saying that death is the cure for the ills of life."

The conversation is now disjointed. Morgan points out that this is the first time Socrates talks about sacrifice and wonders whether this is significant. Kristopher notes that in Greek society libations of wine were poured out to the gods, not libations of poison, and also wonders whether this is significant. The other Christopher thinks that issues of life and death are not under Socrates' control and therefore he turns to the gods.

At this point I am going crazy because I so want to respond to this question, and I wish that I were not hamstrung by my self-imposed silence. The *Phaedo* has struck something deep inside my soul.

As much as Socrates was a gadfly, this poignant and touching dialogue is about an innocent man who is facing imminent death. He comforts himself with the knowledge that the world in which he lives is fleeting and that in death his soul will live on, finally to know true justice and beauty.

Of course, this is a difficult concept for my classmates to really understand because most of them have never had to confront death. Teenagers think that they will live forever. But I *have* faced death, so I am reading Socrates' last words in a very different way than my classmates.

To me, the *Phaedo* is about courage. It's about victory over death. It is a work that someone who has AIDS can find comfort in. It is a work that a prisoner of war facing torture can understand. It is a work that speaks poignantly to a patient in a hospital dying of cancer, because Socrates comforts us with the knowledge that a better world awaits us after we leave this one.

As I read *Phaedo* and consider Socrates' plight, I think back to the summer of 2000, when my oncologist in Virginia told me I had a year to live. Back to the anxieties that ran through my mind about dying, about my daughters' education, and about Susan. Back to my first meeting with William Sharfman, one of the country's leading melanoma experts, who enrolled me in a treatment program at Johns Hopkins. And, finally, back to my room in Weinberg, where I was constantly in pain and vomiting frequently from the exotic cocktail of Interleukin II, Velban, Dacarbazine, and Cisplatin I was receiving through the catheter in my chest. In my mind's eye I was at the edge of death. I wasn't sure I wanted to live if it meant that my body would be consumed by this horrible disease. Subliminally, I needed a modern-day Asclepius to put me out of my misery.

But this was not how it ended for me.

My treatment worked! I was a complete responder. I would live. So now I owe a proverbial cock to Asclepius, not for a poison that might have ended my life, but rather in gratitude to God and to the doctors and the medicine that saved me.

· · ·

I am being interviewed over dinner at the Ram's Head Tavern by Rob Hiaasen, the *Baltimore Sun* columnist. The Ram's Head is a St. John's hangout and where I imagine the Johnnies who skip the Friday night lecture come to surreptitiously hoist a pint or two. At the ample bar in the front are many varieties of ale on tap, several of which are handcrafted in a brewhouse next door. It's still early, but in a couple of hours the bar will be jampacked with college kids, not just St. John's students, but also upper-class midshipmen from the Naval Academy disguised in civilian clothes. Rob and I are seated in the back room eating crab cakes and fried oysters.

Six feet, two inches tall, Rob was an athlete in school. Fascinated by my sabbatical, he is doing an in-depth story for his column. "Come on, Roger," he is saying between bites of his crab cake, echoing what other reporters have been asking me. "What could a college president possibly learn by becoming a freshman again? Why did you *really* do this?"

Rob's question strikes a chord. At Occoquan, when I was rowing at an exhausting pace to the starting point of our race, I was asking myself this same question. But at the end of the race, in that moment when oxygen was flooding back into my semi-delirious brain and I was regaining full consciousness, and later, as I read the *Phaedo*, I began to understand not only why I had gone out for crew, but also why I had taken this crazy sabbatical.

My victory on the Occoquan Reservoir was more than just a boat race for me. Four years before, I had been given the gift of life when I beat a deadly cancer. I now needed to prove to myself that I still had a future, that I wasn't on a treadmill going nowhere. That even in my sixties I could grow into a different person. For me, then, Occoquan represented a victory over aging and the fear we all have that our lives will be over when we retire. I proved that even in the evening of my life, I could go back to college and learn new things. That I could enjoy the company of men and women decades younger than myself and become a part of their community. That I could even row in a boat with eight teenagers. In short, I discovered that my life wasn't winding down, as perhaps I thought it was when I was in Weinberg, but in many ways it was just beginning, with a refreshed sense of commitment and confidence in what I could be. I had been in Plato's cave, unfocused and unsettled, seeing only the shadows of my previous life. I was ready to give up and die. But my freshman semester at St. John's, culminating in this personal victory at Occoquan, allowed me to see a new light, a new reality, a new life.

This victory at Occoquan also represented a victory over life's routines. For me, being a college president meant being in control, telling people what to do, and having a tight grip on everything. But what I learned at St. John's is that I would enjoy life much more if I loosened that grip and became less imperious and controlling. I learned this both from Mr. Pickens and from my daughter, Kate, whose advice to relax and let the oar handle rest loosely in my hands quickly became a mantra for my new life. But I also learned this lesson in seminar, where I had to listen rather than speak. The art of listening is often lost on college presidents like me, and I discovered that I would be a better leader if I sometimes kept my mouth shut and my ears open.

Finally, my entire freshman semester was really a victory for the liberal arts and sciences. I have always known that the best preparation for careers in our increasingly high-tech society is a liberal arts education. What I didn't fully appreciate until I came to St. John's is that a liberal arts education is with us *forever*. Little did I realize at the time that both Denison and Drew were giving me the intellectual tools that would set me up for a lifetime of learning, the most recent episode taking place right here in Annapolis. I discovered that I could read the great works of Homer, Plato, and Herodotus in ways that would give new meaning to my life. Homer gave me a better understanding of homesickness and the insecurities of my youth. Plato spoke to my more recent encounter with death. And, of course, Herodotus led me to a deeper appreciation for what it means to be a historian.

As I reflect on Rob Hiaasen's question and on the greater meaning of this victory at Occoquan, I am reminded of President Nelson's convocation address way back in August. He told the freshmen on that sunny morning that we had embarked on a wonderful journey, one that would begin over and over again throughout our lives. He said that even if our journey and the search it entailed had taken us to a secure landing as college students, this landing was only the jumping-off point for another journey, for a further search. He ended by telling us that the goal of this search was to return and, for the first time, know the place from whence we started.

Being able to understand, perhaps for the first time, the meaning of my past life, and, more importantly, discovering what life still has in store for me is the *real* reason I took this strange but wonderful sabbatical.

NOT TOOK —

It's what he learned

Epilogue

As we sit around the seminar table during our final meeting before winter break, my classmates look extremely tired. They
have just finished reading and discussing Thucydides' *Peloponnesian War,* a companion piece to Herodotus's *History.* Whereas
Herodotus deals with the rise and fall of Persia during its un-
successful invasion of Greece, Thucydides discusses the subse-
quent disintegration of Greece itself when the various Greek
states—Athens and Sparta foremost among them—engage in
internecine warfare. The *Peloponnesian War* is about misguided
national ambition and can be read with great profit against the
background of European colonial ventures in the nineteenth
century and America's new role as the world's only superpower
in the twenty-first century. The book is long and exhausting to
read, and as much as we enjoy it, semester break and the holi-
days are very much on our minds.

But one last pleasure awaits us, namely, Plato's *Symposium.*
For the past several weeks we have been told by our tutors as

well as upperclassmen that the *Symposium* is not only loads of fun to read and discuss, but also serves as a proper send-off for winter break.

The *Symposium* begins at a drinking party—an event very familiar to college students—in the home of Agathon, a friend of Plato. The party takes place well before Socrates' trial and death, and includes on the guest list some of Athens's most illustrious philosophers and statesmen, including the comic poet Aristophanes, the statesman Alcibiades, and, of course, Socrates himself.

Near the beginning of the *Symposium,* the physician Eryximachus makes an eloquent speech about drinking to excess, a speech that I am sure is not lost on the members of my seminar. "If I have learned anything from medicine," Eryximachus preaches to his fellow partygoers, "it is the following point: inebriation is harmful to everyone. Personally, therefore, I always refrain from heavy drinking; and I advise others against it— especially people who are suffering the effects of the previous night's excesses" (Plato *Symposium* 176d). As a result of Eryximachus's speech, the group collectively decides not to get drunk, as they often do on these occasions, but instead to engage in a mostly serious conversation about the meaning of love, or "eros."

The speeches begin with Phaedrus, an Athenian orator, and end with Alcibiades, the Greek statesman and general. The speeches are a mixed bag. Some make complete sense to my classmates, while others, quite frankly, are over the top and rather disturbing.

Eryximachus himself speaks of love in a clinical way, as a physician or a scientist might, analyzing love in its healthy and diseased states. Aristophanes, whose play *The Clouds,* a humorous parody of Socrates, was previously read by our seminar, describes heterosexual and homosexual love using the bizarre imagery of four-legged circles, some male, some female, and some androgynous. When Socrates' turn comes, he, of course, talks about a more ephemeral, ideal kind of love. Quoting a wise woman by the name of Diotima, Socrates describes love as "wanting to possess the good forever" and as "beautiful itself, absolute, pure, unmixed, not polluted by human flesh" (ibid. 206a, 211e).

Responding to Mrs. Kronsberg's question about whether there is a tension in the *Symposium* between physical love and the love of wisdom, Christopher walks up to the blackboard and draws a ladder, labeling the lower rung "physical love" and the top rung "love of the soul." "We all start out seeking someone who is physically beautiful," Christopher says as he points to the lower rungs of the ladder, "but then move up the ladder seeking higher forms of love and beauty."

As Christopher delivers this impromptu lecture, I am thinking about how my feelings for the young men and women sitting around this table have grown over time into a deep and abiding love for each one of them. The Pauline concept of "agape" best describes the kind of love I am trying to describe, a concept these students will learn about next year when they read and discuss the Bible.

The first day of seminar these students were nameless people whom I identified by their physical attributes, including their tattoos, nose rings, beards, and apparel. Soon enough, however, they became human beings with names and unique qualities. The kid with the Amish-style beard became Seth, whose wisecracks in class made me laugh. The young woman with the rose tattoo on her shoulder became Alyssa, whose insight into children and family I came to appreciate. The guy with the shaved head and silver earrings became Sebastian, a young man whose depth of thought and perception captivated the entire seminar. And the young man wearing a Hawaiian shirt decorated with tropical flowers became Justin, my teammate and good friend.

Had I been at Agathon's party, I probably would have made a speech as well, about how each of these young men and women has touched my life in a deep and meaningful way. About how I looked forward to sitting next to Zach, the roly-poly kid who always gave me a warm greeting when I entered the seminar room. About how I anticipated Elizabeth's feminist comments whenever women were mistreated in the literature we were reading—which was frequently. About how I enjoyed Christopher's insightful comments about the more difficult passages we struggled with. About how Morgan's sometimes fiery repartee with the tutors kept the conversation around the table lively. I would tell Socrates and Aristophanes and the others that these young students and the young students like them that I have known over the thirty years I have been in higher education have made my life worth living. I would tell them, in the best way I could, that the bond between student and teacher, when together they explore wisdom and justice and virtue, is perhaps the highest, the most noble, the most perfect form of love there can be.

. . .

This is what I would have said if I had been invited to Agathon's party. Tonight I attend a different kind of party. It's called the Winter Collegium, and it marks the end of the fall term for St. John's students. For me it marks the end of my time at St. John's as well.

Collegium, much like the Waltz Parties and Friday night lectures, is a St. John's tradition that one doesn't want to miss. It is an all-college musical celebration, followed by the assistant dean's holiday party, followed in turn by an end-of-semester Waltz Party. Since several of my classmates are performing, I know I must attend.

I arrive late, entering the Great Hall by the same side door I tiptoed into when I showed up for chorus. The Great Hall is packed from top to bottom. As I edge my way to the upper-floor balcony, overlooking the area where I once attended waltz lessons, a student named Ali is standing next to a baby grand piano singing "Lascia ch'io pianga," from the opera *Rinaldo*. I do a double take. Playing the piano is none other than Henry from crew, the human submarine. Several more students then perform a variety of songs and acts to an enthusiastic audience made up mostly of classmates, but also including some faculty. I see Christian Holland on the other side of the balcony.

A junior by the name of Arthur is now belting out "La vie en rose," which he dedicates to his French tutor, telling the audience before he begins that if they applaud loudly enough at the conclusion, he might get some extra credit. Of course he brings the house down when he finishes. Soon Tim, my classmate from seminar, is on stage, ready to play the violin. In the beginning of seminar I was not very impressed with Tim, who seemed somewhat nervous and inarticulate. Soon, however, I was moved by his intelligent and often perceptive comments. And here he is now, all dressed up in a jacket and tie, playing the Allemanda from Bach's Partita in D Minor for Solo Violin before a crowd of his peers. What a guy!

The entertainment ends with a surprise. The St. John's Community Chorus, with Peter Kalkavage directing, is about to perform. This is the same choral group I intended to join when I arrived at St. John's but unceremoniously gave up for crew. I look down from the balcony and spot the very same student with the English accent who not only was my dance instructor at waltz lessons, but also beckoned me to pull up a seat when, back in early September, I arrived late for choir practice. Now she seems to be looking up at me and thinking to herself, "If you had followed my advice, you could be singing with us right now. Too bad."

The chorus begins to sing in Latin, first *Salve Regina* and then *Locus iste,* the two pieces I once rehearsed with them. Their presence brings me full circle, from my arrival at St. John's four months ago to my planned departure two days from now.

The concert is over, and now there is a brief interlude before the assistant dean's holiday party begins. I spot Justin, who is leaning against the balcony railing, and go over to chat with him. Right from the beginning of my time here, Justin has been easy for me to talk to, and our common experiences at crew and in seminar have only made our conversations even more enjoyable. He tells me that he will miss the last meeting of seminar tomorrow in order to catch a flight back to Honolulu. It's 22 degrees outside, and I joke that the real reason he is going home so early is so that he can avoid the frigid weather of Annapolis.

"So, Justin," I ask him, "what *is* the temperature in Honolulu right now?"

"You don't want to know, Roger," he responds with a whimsical smile.

The holiday party is now starting up. Students and faculty have gravitated to the refreshment table at the west end of the Great Hall, where song sheets with holiday carols are handed out. But before I can get to the table, a student I have never seen before approaches me.

"President Martin," she says, "my name is Semantha. I'm a junior, and I'm planning to attend Oxford after I graduate next year. I understand you went there, and I wonder if you can give me some advice." At Randolph-Macon this would be a normal occurrence. Students often ask me for suggestions or for advice about graduate school. But while I am happy to discuss these things with Semantha, it once again occurs to me that ever since the *Washington Post* article appeared several weeks ago, my status at St. John's has changed from that of a college student to that of a college president. I am no longer "Roger" or even "Mr. Martin," but now "President Martin." I welcome this young woman's approach, but I am more than a little sad that I have lost my identity as a freshman.

As our conversation winds down, I can hear the group beginning to sing holiday carols. Semantha, seeing that I don't have sheet music, invites me to join some of her friends standing on the other side of the room. And there we all are, some three hundred students, a good part of the student body and many faculty and staff as well, all singing carols. And then something quite extraordinary happens.

The sheet music is put away and the entire room—freshmen, sophomores, juniors, and seniors—begins singing Palestrina's *Sicut cervus* in harmony. I have never heard anything like this before. On cue, the diverse St. John's community is singing beautiful a cappella music everyone knows by heart, and I am the only one in the whole pack who doesn't know the words.

I remember the "great misunderstanding" between Ms. Seeger and myself. Back in August she had encouraged me to sing in the chorus, but I had misunderstood, thinking that she was encouraging me to sing in one of the community choral programs. Only when Annie told me several weeks ago that freshman chorus was her favorite subject did I realize that I had tried to join the wrong choral group. To my deep regret, I have missed out on a wonderful part of the St. John's freshman experience. I am aware of no other college that requires its students, even those who cannot sing, to participate in a choral program as St. John's does. So I just stand to the side of the Great Hall and listen to the beautiful singing, with a tear in my eye. I see so many young friends from seminar and crew, and I feel an intimate part of this wonderful community. I feel blessed that I have been invited into their lives.

.   .   .

The evening ends with a Waltz Party. It's now 11 P.M., and about seventy-five students remain in the Great Hall. Of these, fifty are swing dancing. I see Katrina, from my seminar, dancing with Jack, from my boat. Over there is Thom, stroke in my boat, cutting the rug with Eleanor, the South African student, as though the world were coming to an end. Victoria, normally so quiet and sedate, is doing the swing with Phil, who, God bless him, is not only wearing something besides his University of Pennsylvania sweatshirt, but is sporting a cologne I can smell from across the room. He waves. I see Jessie and Morgan and Emily from seminar, all sitting off to the side of the room and engaged in animated conversation with Shannon. I wonder whether they are discussing the *Symposium*. I don't see Sheldon, though, and this makes me sad. He left for California last week, unable even to finish the last few days of class. A note he sent to my house on Franklin Street tells me how much I meant to him and how bad he feels about leaving St. John's under such difficult circumstances.

As the music gets louder, the portraits of past St. John's presidents hanging on the walls of the Great Hall—including one of Stringfellow Barr, who helped institute the Great Books curriculum back in the 1930s—are swaying back and forth. As I watch this happen I have an eerie feeling, a sensation of unusual continuity. For the past several months I have been part of a dynamic community that antedates the signing of our Constitution. And as I stand in this room, deep in thought, I feel part of something very special.

It's now almost midnight, and even the noise can't keep me awake. And so I slip out of the Great Hall and walk home to Franklin Street one last time.

BIBLIOGRAPHY

Aeschylus. *The Oresteia*. Translated by Robert Fagles. New York: Penguin Books, 1979.

―――. *The Oresteia*. Translated by Hugh Lloyd-Jones. Berkeley: University of California Press, 1994.

Herodotus. *The History*. Translated by George Rawlinson. Chicago: Encyclopaedia Britannica, 1955.

―――. *The History*. Translated by David Grene. Chicago: University of Chicago Press, 1987.

Homer. *The Iliad*. Translated by Robert Fagles. New York: Penguin Books, 1998.

―――. *The Odyssey*. Translated by Robert Fagles. New York: Penguin Books, 1997.

Plato. *Apology*. Translated by G. M. A. Grube. In *Plato Complete Works*, ed. J. M. Cooper. Indianapolis: Hackett, 1997.

―――. *Crito*. Translated by G. M. A. Grube. In *Plato Complete Works*.

―――. *Gorgias*. Translated by D. J. Zeyl. In *Plato Complete Works*.

―――. *The Republic*. Translated by G. M. A. Grube. In *Plato Complete Works*.

————. *Symposium*. Translated by Alexander Nehamas and Paul Woodruff. In *Plato Complete Works*.

Thucydides. *The Peloponnesian War*. Translated by Steven Lattimore. Indianapolis: Hackett, 1998.